CROSS-COUNTRY SKIING
IN NEW ENGLAND

"Just thumbing through the pages of this guidebook gives you the feeling that the authors have really explored the places they describe."
—Maine *Sunday Telegram*

"Notes in its introduction that children are welcome at all of the ski areas included in the guide."
—*Family Travel Times*

"This book is the next best thing to a guide at your side."
—*The New England Sampler*, Belfast, Maine

CROSS-COUNTRY SKIING IN NEW ENGLAND

Third Edition

by
Lyn and Tony Chamberlain

Photography by Janet Knott

The Globe Pequot Press

Old Saybrook, Connecticut

Photo on pages 2 and 71 by Steven Stagnitti (courtesy of the Trapp Family Lodge); page 143 copyright © 1989 by Peter Miller (courtesy of the Trapp Family Lodge). All other photos by Janet Knott.

Library of Congress Cataloging-in-Publication Data

Chamberlain, Lyn.
    Cross-country skiing in New England/by Lyn and Tony Chamberlain.
    —3rd ed.
        p.   cm.
    Includes index.
    ISBN 1-56440-056-5
    1. Cross-country-skiing—New England—Guidebooks. 2. New England—Guidebooks. I. Chamberlain, Tony. II. Title.
GV854.5.N35C45 1992

                                                                92-8765
                                                                CIP

Manufactured in the United States of America
Third Edition/First Printing

for Earl and Hobie,
with our love

CONTENTS

Prologue: One of Too Few Days 1

Introduction 9
   About This Book   9
   A Few Misconceptions   12
   To the Downhill Skier   16
   Beyond the Good News   19
   Off to the Races   19
   That Question: Wax   23
   Skating   30
   What to Wear   31

Connecticut 33
   Map   34
Massachusetts 41
   Map   42
Vermont 61
   Map   62
New Hampshire 117
   Map   118
Maine 147
   Map   148

Index to Skiing Sites 177

Prologue:
One of Too Few Days

It was nearly 4 A.M. and the wind was down. Whatever had woken me—there were mice in this place, we knew—was still now. I went over to the window and pulled back the wool blanket we had tacked against the cold early last evening. When we turned in, a storm was raging across the valley, so the window was just a flat black. But sometime in the night the weather had blown itself out. Now, over the still silver landscape, hung a solemn January moon. I knew in a few hours one of Those Days was going to dawn.

There are too few such days in a winter; too few in a lifetime. The world remade by new snow, bright sun in an endless sky (for the high pressure was surely locked in for a while), and no commitment beyond a full day's skiing. It would be perfect. Even anticipating such a day, knowing how brief and finite it would be, brought a peculiar sense of dread to underline the exhilaration as I stood there at the window. I thought thoughts that look grotesquely sentimental on paper:

"This would be a day to be tuned to every minute, to resist that all-too-human habit of blocking off the senses, of losing awareness so that hours of light slip by uncounted, practically unnoticed.

"That may be okay back in the work world, sitting in commuter traffic or something of the kind. But not this day. This day would be perfect, every minute of it to be turned over and over, examined, savored."

Three hours later the moon was down and the first streak of hard orange light slashed across the peak of Bald Mountain. Bacon and coffee smells filled the cabin; during twenty years of marriage, these two chores—the spadework of our vacation breakfasts—have fallen to me. Then Lyn, the superstar surgeon who can flip fried eggs without breaking them, steps in for the artistic work.

You can eat a big breakfast before a day of skiing, for the sport burns calories like none other I know. We were staying at a friend's camp in northern Maine, and the plan was to ski 12 miles to a village at the far shore of the lake, then cross the lake for a 4-mile shot home. After breakfast, as Lyn packed a trail lunch, I went about the ceremonial business of determining the wax of the day.

I have been with ski groups who delight in arguing all through breakfast about waxing, various members going out every five minutes to stick a thermometer in sunlit snow, then in the shady snow, then to stand around ruminatively stroking their chins while pretending to know a great deal about winter. My own experience is that for recreational touring you can be a color or so off to the cold side and it really won't matter much, especially if your touch on the skis is right. All it will really mean is that you herringbone uphill a little sooner than you would otherwise. And you can be more than a color off to the warm side before you start clogging up your kick zone.

I used some paint thinner to remove some old grip wax from the green glider base we'd ironed on the fiber glass bottoms at the beginning of the season, then on the kick zone I smeared some green grip wax—just a guess on my part about what would be a good start in this dry, fluffy stuff.

Anyway, as long as waxing stays ceremonial, it is fun. So the skis were prepared on our perfect morning, lunch, waxes, extra clothes packed in the back pack, and off we went.

The empty woods on a cold morning ring with quiet. The powder was still unbroken as we made our way up behind the cabin, mounting toward a high ridge that ran for about 3 miles overlooking the lake. The only breaks in the trail were the delicate strings of beads, the tracks of small animals—squirrels, snowshoe hare, voles, and the like—up and busy in these hills long before us. During a blizzard deer will hunker down in the snow and become buried for the duration. When they sense the storm's end, they will break out to continue their ceaseless winter foraging for food, and you sometimes come upon their tracks on winter mornings after a snowfall. You are reminded that northern New England is the extreme range of whitetail deer; in the deepest months the animals are always in peril.

As you stretch out, skiing faster through the dark hollows and over small rises—always ascending—the muscles work out, and the stiffness of beginning is gone. Skiing becomes easier. You are in rhythm and are aware of your sound, skis patting, then gliding on the snow, your breath coming out in plumes as your lungs work to drink the winter-cold oxygen. Rhythm, the slash-slash of skis, the steamy breath, and suddenly you become aware of how lound the sound of your skiing is in this early silence.

Still in shade, we made one slight descent, then turned uphill again through a stand of birch and snow-laden fir boughs. I chose one route up here; Lyn said she would skirt around through another likely looking road that would be better going and would meet me at the other side of a knoll I was already ascending.

"I think my way's shorter," I told her.

"It's too thick-looking up there. I'm taking the road," she said, and we parted company.

I was determined to get over the knoll, then ski back down the road, to be waiting there not even breathing hard, as if I'd been there for half the morning when she showed up. Skiing harder up toward the rise, I had to duck under several branches so heavily laden they looked ready to snap. As my shoulder brushed by, unburdening them, the boughs sprung one by one toward the sky, spraying me with powder.

Toward the top of a mountain ridge, summer or winter, when you emerge from thick woods to a spacious overlook, there is a sense of climbing out a skylight onto the roof of the world. Here, abruptly, I was in sunlight, full and dazzling. Far below, the lake spread out for 10 miles, a pool of spilled milk. Beyond one shore, the tiny village stoked its fires in the cold morning, the thin curls of smoke rising from every rooftop into the valley air. Even farther beyond the lake and village rose another mountain ridge, then another a fainter blue behind it, and another behind that. Looking out over moutain ranges, you can see the tumultuous energy of a frozen ocean. And as far as I could see, perhaps 80 miles, just visible behind the last ridge rose the oddly sinister white bulk of Mountain Katahdin.

It was some time before I noticed there was no way down from where I stood. The underbrush among the firs down the sunny side of the ridge was waist-high and so thick there was no apparent opening. But I was not about the backtrack to the road, then skirt all the way around, following Lyn by perhaps fifteen minutes. I drove down through the underbrush and commenced such a fight with the thickets that, after ten minutes or so, I was more amused than irritated. I would hack an opening and make a move through it, only to find that one ski was so hung up around a stalk or some creeper vines that I must back up again, then look to the other ski to see what it was doing. Meanwhile, I had to duck under the heavy fir boughs that kept dumping their powder over my shoulders and head. Just as I was losing a ridiculous battle with these woods, I was at last free and worked down to the road. As I arrived, snow-covered, disheveled, steaming and panting from the effort, there was Lyn looking as if she'd been waiting there all morning. No explanation was necessary. "How's the other guy look?" she asked.

We found a patch of sunlight to stop in. After two hours of skiing, it was time to shed a layer and have some coffee and Hershey chunks, before pushing on to our lunch stop. We descended half a mile to the lake. Where the downhill run was clear, it was exhilarating, for we could let out the skis as fast as we could travel through powder, then slow down naturally as the terrain leveled. But it did occur to me that going downhill on skinny skis is not as much fun as going up gentle climbs, or over flats. And this is a matter of sheer skiing skill, or lack thereof: You can learn to charge over flats and pump uphill and get the same exhilarating high that distance runners feel. But the ability to ride a ski downhill with confidence through twisting terrain and switchbacks—that is a matter of years and miles under the skis. For that there is no substitute.

Our lunch was hot soup from a wide-mouth Thermos, chicken chunks, bread, cheese, and wine to wash it down. Now the sun was high and flooded into our small clearing. I peeled off a layer and sat there steaming, pointing my face stupidly to the sky. Odd, wasn't it? Here in the heart of winter—the darkest month in one of the fiercest climates in North America—it was possible to peel off layers of clothing, sip wine, and nearly doze in the sunshine. But shadows begin to elongate quickly on a January day. After half an hour or so there was a sudden nudge of urgency. Get going. We picked up, smeared a touch of blue wax over the green, and were off again, feeling stiff and cranky, along the shore of the lake.

We were getting near civilization now. The first sign was the waste of raw material from which the outlanders—beavers— had built winter communes. They had built two huge lodges just offshore of the lake, and all along the shore lay the ruins of birch trees they had felled for the construction. A wasteful project, this, for the beavers used only medium logs and small limbs, leaving the greater part of the tree sprawled on the forest floor to rot. And how much more wasteful, it seems, when the waste is birch. Scattered among these stands of beech, maple, and birch were silver birches, the prettiest trees I have seen, their trunks shining a bright gold-bronze color, bright as polished metal in the chilly sunlight.

We passed out of beaver country and began coming upon the most common of lodgings in ski country, the ubiquitous, inevitable condominium. With the first ones we passed, we knew, despite the last part of our trip ahead of us—a straight shot home across the lake after picking up groceries—The Day was at its end.

And the run home, our dividend, was nearly uneventful except for the hugest of events. Two of them.

Loaded down with two extra packs stuffed with all kinds of unnecessaries for the rest of our week up-country, we headed back across the lake just as the sun diffused in the broad florid band across the western sky, an unconvincing final show of force before the winter night shut down over all light once again. It was comfortable on the lake. There was no wind. Skiers had left behind plenty of tracks for us to get into and cruise along, and the dropping temperature made the surface firm and fast. And again there was the exhilaration of the aerobic rhythm, the rhythm of motion and breathing, that slash-slash of the skis. We were across in no time.

We ascended the opposite banking crossing a neighbor's meadow in the dark, then up past his barn where a solitary

white cat dozed on a window ledge under the outside light. Then into the dark again, through more trees to the last field we would have to cross to get back to our cabin. At the edge of the clearing there was movement of some kind. Startled, I stared at something large and dark moving against the trees. The movement was not rushed, but slow and weighty. I was stunned. I tried to focus on an oft-repeated belief of an old Vermonter who taught me how to fly-fish: "The only animal you have to worry about in the New England woods stands on two legs."

Then I thought the neighbor's cows or perhaps his horses were loose. But the apparition finally resolved itself into a couple of moose sauntering along at the edge of the woods. If our sudden presence stirred them into motion, they certainly were not hurried about anything now. Their heads looking naked without antlers—the winter style for these thousand-pound monsters—they slowly shuffled toward the trees. Moose are the only creatures in New England for whom winter absolutely does not exist. I have seen them from an airplane lying on their backs and wriggling back and forth like horses in summer mud. Where the whitetailed deer are constantly threatened up here, these huge cousins do not even feel the pinch.

We heard their hooves plunge lazily a few times, then the noise stopped. The moose had stopped just a few yards into the trees and would wait for us to pass on before coming back to the clearing. It is no wonder hunters have a 90-percent success ratio up here with these brutes.

We crossed the last field, slowly and sorely now; day's end was suddenly long overdue. Halfway across the field we could see that the friends we'd expected sometime that evening had already arrived and were waiting for us. The windows were full of light. You could see wood smoke from the chimney against the stars.

Introduction

This book has been assembled with the single purpose of enhancing the pleasure of cross-country skiers in their sport by pointing them in certain directions. It by no means pretends to be a skiing bible. It does not get especially technical in questions of technique, and it even waffles on the question of whether to buy waxable or waxless skis. Its waxing approach is clearly for the lazy. It does not tell you how to skate or double-pole. It does not even attempt to suggest that descending steep turny downhills on Nordic skis will ever be anything but a terror for you.

No, these pages have been assembled by a couple of folks who love the sport of skiing in all its facets, who love the rural reaches of New England and who hardly miss a winter weekend getting there, and who now share with you a few of the things they have found out.

About This Book

This is a guidebook for skiers and has been written for the skier, not the ski area. That is to say, the descriptions of ski areas herein are as faithful to the experience as we could make them. Prospective skiers may be influenced by what they read here to try this touring center or that one because it rings a particular note of appeal. That is the intent of this book.

Certain information may be lacking. Price, for instance. As you look at the statistical top half of an area's description, you will not find price. That is only partly because we hope this book outlives the price changes of one or two years. More to the point, within a 95-percent range of all the areas, prices are all about the same: They fall between $3 and $6 for a day's trail pass. Rental equipment ranges from $8 to $12.

Two other near universals: There are no areas where children are unwelcome; there are no areas where pets are welcome.

Unlike many Alpine areas that make a selling point of the fact that they operate a nursery for toddlers, this is hardly ever the case with Nordic areas. Exceptions will be noted in the narrative section in the lower half of the description.

Dogs? Leave them home, period. You may have a romantic picture in your mind of coursing through the pristine woodlands with Rover leaping along beside you. Save this for woods and wilderness touring of your own making. But when visiting a commercial touring center, especially one with groomed and trackset trails, leave the beasties home. Aside from ruining the track as they run along, dogs will inevitably blunder into the path of another skier (especially on double tracks), and send that skier out of control, or worse, unwittingly knock him over. No fair. Dogs stay home.

A word about trail difficulty. The nomenclature has changed over the years, and the current terms "easiest, more difficult, most difficult" have been thoughtfully chosen by the Professional Ski Instructors of America (PSIA). They replace the earlier "beginner, intermediate, expert" for two important reasons. First, these earlier terms were an attempt to describe the skiers who should use such trails, not the trails themselves. Secondly, no one knows exactly what the terms really mean. What is the difference, please, between an "advanced intermediate" and a newly arrived "expert," or an "experienced beginner"?

The new terms attempt to describe, in a relative way, the difficulty of a particular trail. If a trail system offers "most difficult" terrain, that means it is more difficult than its second-degree terrain, "more difficult." This latter is more difficult than the "easiest" terrain at the particular area, but not necessarily at all areas.

The trail-grooming entry attempts to let a skier know what sort of a playing surface to expect. A groomed trail means that some device or other—perhaps just a snowmobile—has passed over the raw snow and packed it down, making it generally a bit faster and easier to ski than nongroomed snow. A *trackset* is just what it says. By pulling another device over the snow, a firm, well-defined track is set to ski in. This makes the skiing easier and faster and is sought by folks who like to "run" on their skis. On tracks it is easier to concentrate on what your body is doing rather than the terrain.

Double trackset means at least two tracks have been set, one beside another. This works just like automobile traffic (with the exception of one-way loops). Faster skiers pull out to pass slower ones; skiers from opposite directions pass without having to get out of a track. There is nothing less courteous, by the way, than two companion skiers coming abreast of one another, using both tracks, and forcing a skier from the opposite direction out of his right-hand track. Very gauche, but it is mentioned here because it happens. Probably new converts from Alpine skiing.

Under the instruction entry, PSIA-certified stands for Professional Ski Instructors of America. If the notation is made this way it means that your instructor has had to prove to other professional instructors that he knows what he is doing and teaches according to a method recognized and used by all others in PSIA. It is an indication that you will have a skilled teacher.

The converse, however, is decidedly not true. Merely because a teacher is noncertified is no indication that he is not just as good as a certified instructor. So don't weigh this category too heavily, except to note whether any instruction is available.

On rentals, we have noted where possible how many sets are available. Some areas simply chose not to tell us how many they had, while others gave us detailed rundowns on the state-of-the-art binding systems. One rule of thumb anywhere, however: If you're going to rent, show up early. This is obviously true of the busier areas but should be standard practice anyway. Arriving later may mean you're forced into compromises like skis too long and boots too small. No fun. One alternative to explore is renting equipment at the ski shop near your home and taking it with you. This way you'll also avoid the brutal Saturday-morning crush in the rental store.

To know where you're going, use the state map. Find the number of the touring center you are visiting. The number refers to the map index giving you the page number where the area is described. Between the description in the book and the routes on the map, most places will be easy to find. But frequent visitors to New England's rural reaches should also be armed with full-scale, detailed road maps.

Two final notes: First to skiers, this book is written for you. Write and give us feedback. Tell us where you think we blew it. Maybe we glowed too much, or not enough. Perhaps you found some feature worth noting at an area that we missed. The only way we'll ever know is if you drop us a line at The Globe Pequot Press, P.O. Box 833, Old Saybrook, CT 06475.

To the touring centers, if you have made changes or improvements that we should know about, or if we have overlooked an important feature of your center that you feel should be included, likewise, drop us a line.

And to any touring center not included herein, understand that this book is not advertising. No touring center has paid to be listed in this book. If you wish to be considered for a future edition, please write and let us know you're out there.

All that said, we repeat the hope that this guide to skiing in New England will accomplish our single goal of contributing to the pleasures of the marvelous sport of cross-country skiing.

A Few Misconceptions

In the autumn of 1984 Russian archaeologists found a ski near Soviet Georgia carbon-dated to an age of 4,000 B.C. That find displaced by a thousand years a Norwegian ski previously believed to be the oldest in existence. Whatever competitive spirit may exist over what country owns the oldest ski, the real point is that in frigid climes man has probably been on skis as long as he has used his feet. Beyond mere amusement or exercise regimen, the simple fact is that skiing is the fastest, easiest, and natural way to travel over the snow-covered earth.

Not that the sport needs a defense. Indeed, cross-country skiing, with all its names and variants—ski touring, Nordic, Norpine, Telemarking—is here for a good long stay. It has that winning formula: cheap, simple, healthy, and fun. Its importance to a modern human who increasingly searches for ways to bring nature into his recreational and exercise life makes skiing nearly as significant as it was to ancient man.

For a decade in our country, cross-country skiing has redoubled several times in popularity. The sport is now an established, solid, growing, thriving, and incredibly healthful endeavor. But a few old misconceptions still remain.

Number One: It's too much work.

Well, for starters, how much work is too much work? Some people believe cross-country skiing is in the running family—that if they can't imagine themselves jogging 5 miles a day, then they're disqualified from cross-country skiing.

Not so. Running, aside from the well-documented jarring involved, is an all-or-nothing sort of regimen. That is, either one is running or one is not running. If one is not running he is walking or standing still. If he is running, no matter how slowly, he is under terrific stress—the whole point of the sport. His only way out is to stop, and then he is not running anymore.

Skiing is very different in that regard. In its recreational mode it is much more like bicycling. One can bike at 100 beats a minute in the Tour de France, or one can coast and cruise. Pump five strokes, then let the legs rest as the eyes take in the countryside. Skiing can be done exactly this way, from a vigorous running pace to a leisurely cruise with lots of coasting. To be utterly frank, though, if an easy-to-moderately-paced bike ride is too much work for you, then, yes, cross-country skiing is probably not for you, either.

Number Two: It's boring.

This is easier. Anyone who gets bored with the winter wilderness outside those walls, with the dazzle of sun on snow-white and evergreen, is simply bored with himself, bored with life, we think. Cross-country skiing won't help.

Number Three: If you can walk you can cross-country ski.

We have seen too many people disappointed by this amiably misguided notion to let it go unanswered. There is a minimal amount of truth here to be sure. The phrase is generally repeated to assure novices that Nordic skiing has nothing of the slam-bang recklessness they perceive in downhill skiing.

In some ways this is true, but it is only true because you begin to cross-country ski on flat terrain. Move the legs in a walking sort of way, and you will move forward. No problem. But somewhere along the way one of two things will happen. The new skier will eventually encounter the need to go up, down, or sideways—situations that call for more concentration than your average after-dinner walk. Or, as he steps along, another skier will go by him on the trail so fast he looks motor-driven. Actually, this skilled skier looks like a little machine put together with elastic bands and pendulums: everything rhythmic, easy, and—oh Lord!—so fast.

Once the new cross-country skier sees what real skiing is like, he endeavors to go faster, mainly because the faster you go on skis the more fun you have. But it takes more skill to go fast, as well as some practice and experience. It is here that cross-country skiing departs the realm of walking. Oh, it is still as leisurely as the skier wants it to be. But once the bug gets into the advanced beginner's head that springing across flat tracks at 15 miles an hour looks like fun, well, in our judgment that is the real gateway to cross-country fun. And it sure isn't walking then.

How to get from here to there?

That's the easiest question in the book. Take a lesson. Get a certified professional to teach you. Not in big doses. But half an hour here, half an hour there. The practice in-between times—pleasant miles under the skis—-is the key to progressing. Keep in mind, however, that you do not have to progress, but you will most likely want to improve your skills. You need never feel compelled to be anything beyond a woods-walker, an air-sniffer, and birdsong-listener. Indeed, we should all remember that this is primal in the joy of ski touring.

We have seen at least two distinct kinds of malaise develop over this matter of skiing proficiency or skill. One day we took a friend skiing for the first time. He was an athlete, a marathon runner, and a sometime Alpine skier in terrific physical condition. As our appointed date at the Weston Ski Track approached, we made the mistake of sloughing off my friend's real concerns about his first experience with skinny skis.

Would it feel awkward? Would he fall down a lot? Hurt
himself?

"Are you kidding?" we would say, "An athlete in your condition, who has good downhill experience? You'll pick it up
like that."

Our afternoon at Weston was a disaster. Not that our friend
fell all over the place, hurt himself, or hyperventilated in fa-
tigue, mind you. No, cross-country skiing was merely a mad-
dening frustration for him.

At the Weston track there are always a few expert runners
in training who make 20 miles an hour over the flats look easy.
And of course, given our advanced promotion, along with our
friend's expectation that he could master Nordic skiing imme-
diately, well . . . disaster is the word. He teetered unsurely,
tried with determination to take off at top speed, and just never
got over feeling off-balance and rather foolish. A conspicuous
failure. The worst of it was he wanted to look like the experts,
wanted to go just as fast. He thought he should be able to and
just could not understand why it didn't come to him at once.
He has not been skiing since.

The second type of malaise developed in someone we know
who did not want to go fast, who did not want to run through
courses, who cared not a fig about double-poling and less about
skating. If a hill looked less like a challenge than a chore, she
would opt for the route around it. Or at least she would climb
it slowly and under protest.

What she loved most about skiing was the solitude, the
utter porcelain beauty of the winter landscape, the tracks of
wild animals crossing the trail, the difference between white
and silver birch. This woman was (dubiously) blessed with a
husband and two sons who were jocks. Every minute on skis
was a contest with each other or any surrounding bit of landscape. Every ski trip became, rather than a tour in remote
wilderness beauty, a challenge. Where she did not want to run
up a hill, they prodded her with the old, "It'll feel good when
you get up there."

The challenges the males of this family found fun and exciting were merely obstacles to the woman's enjoyment. She
had a feeling they all moved so fast they couldn't possibly take
in their surroundings.

But, you say, understanding this is merely human courtesy or sensitivity.

Yes, of course, as was true in the first case. Still, these are two examples we've seen played out repeatedly. Which is why we invariably suggest that the beginner go straight to a qualified professional instructor. The pro will find out what you know about skiing, what you expect from the sport, and where you want to go. And, he can reassure you that you needn't go anywhere you do not choose to go. He will encourage you to progress at your own pace so you do not frustrate yourself trying to accomplish things you're not ready for.

Friends and relatives who know something about the sport can be helpful, but the truth is they often are not. Often, in fact, they make the cardinal mistake of trying to teach too much, and this leads to serious trouble. Go with the pro. Learn a couple of things every so often to work on when you're skiing at your leisure. And—most important at times—declare yourself to those around you. Don't be bullied into skiing over your head.

To the Downhill Skier

That cross-country skiing has long outlived its critics is no historical accident.

For starters, despite the electric thrill of Alpine skiing, the Nordic version has the advantage of being cheaper, more accessible, more sociable, better exercise, and certainly less crowded. Have you ever stood in a line to take off across a field or golf course for a morning cross-country run?

Not that this book intends to make a judgment of one over the other. Certainly, any skier who understands the heritage of the skimeister gives equal dignity to all forms of the sport. What is best about the ski age we live in is that we need not choose one over the other. The thrill of downhill skiing at high speed with those sure, crisp, steel-edged turns is undeniable. But if the last two decades have proved anything in the entire world of skiing it is that Nordic, cross-country, ski touring, running—whatever term you use to identify the sport—is surely as exciting in its own right and needn't be apologized for as "the alternative."

At the National Cross-Country Championships at Bretton Woods, New Hampshire, in 1982, Tony asked Bill Koch, that year's World Cup winner, what seemed at the time an overly simplistic question: "What separates the winners from the near-winners in this sport of cross-country? Training? Determination? The right wax?"

Koch thought for a moment, assessing his season, then answered in his characteriscally humble way. "I've been doing well on the downhill sections," he said.

His coach, Mike Gallagher, explained more fully. All the skiers in the very top of a world-class field are in peak condition. They've probably waxed the same, and surely all of them on that level are lion-hearted athletes. But Koch's success that year came from his greatness as a downhill skier. Touch, technique, the way he rode his skis so aggressively into turns, flying downhill without the slightest tendency to hold back—it was the great downhiller in Koch that made the great skier and champion.

On the very next day, after the races, a gang of us went up to try the Bretton Woods NASTAR course on an Alpine slope.

We were on Alpine skis. The clear winner among us through twenty-five slalom gates was Craig Ward, a member of the U.S. Nordic team who did the course on cross-country skis. And his were not the steel-edged, fatter compromise called a Norpine ski, either. Ward had skied the course on his light, stiff racing skis that usually require an act of God for us ordinary skiers to turn.

The point is that skiing is skiing is skiing. The division one supposes to exists between Nordic and Alpine forms is at best a thin cultural bias carried on by crabby folks who don't really understand skiing in its broadest sense.

We are in an age of such increasing expense in Alpine skiing that mixing the forms up is becoming ever more popular for the weekend ski family. It's a natural: A day of downhill, a day of cross-country. Actually, the other way around is probably better, since Saturdays are usually more crowded at Alpine areas than are Sundays.

What most downhill skiers find is that rather than a cheap pastime as an alternative, Nordic is a workout that requires the same principles of balance, counter-rotation of the body, leaning well out over the skis, knees bent in the weight transfer of a Telemark turn. And beyond mere technical differences, Nordic skiing has its own rhythm and beauty, a king of pendular symmetry the Alpine aficionado finds hauntingly familiar.

Several of the Nordic centers described in this book are combined with Alpine areas. From Stowe in Vermont to Waterville Valley, New Hampshire, to Kingfield, Maine, and the Sugarloaf environs, to Berkshire East in Massachusetts—wherever you find Alpine skiing there are bound to be some Nordic tracks nearby.

And so here is an invitation to any downhiller who one day feels just a bit down in the checkbook, who dreads another half-hour liftline, who is sick of fussing with 40 pounds of gear, who cannot bear one more chairlift ride of subarctic wind chills, and who just may long for a day of utter solitude in the winter woods of New England: Give Nordic a try. You can rent gear and buy trail maps, lunch, and a starter lesson all for about the price of a lift ticket. And you just might gain some skills that will make you a better downhiller.

Come on and give it a try. What do you have to lose but your prejudices?

Beyond the Good News

If there is a religious zeal among some cross-country skiers—and we're sure there is—then get ready for the real good
news about the sport. We've always known cross-country skiing is good for body as well as soul. But how good?

Rising head and shoulders above the current wave of fitness
gurus (despite her rather diminutive stature) is Jackie Sorenson,
who did as much as anyone to popularize aerobic conditioning.
Sorenson's facts have never been in question. Here is her latest
calorie line on various physical regimens. If you're a 125-pound
person (extrapolate for your weight) then 30 minutes of moderate walking will burn about 125 calories. If you can swim 30
yards per minute, you'll burn 175 calories in the same half
hour; ditto for ice-skating.

Golf will take care of 160 calories per half hour, and moderate biking will burn 175, too, though strenuous biking will take
care of 275. Now hiking: 185 calories per half hour. Good fast
walking: 230. Into the rough stuff. Racquetball: 350 per half
hour, with running pushing close to that figure, depending on
how hard you pump the legs, of course.

We're sure you've guessed what's on the very top of this list.
The heaviest calorie-burning sport of them all is that four-legged
running routine called cross-country skiing. Per half hour, for a
125-pound person (a little person, really) the burn is 500 calories, with the effect all aerobic athletes know well—a high-
calorie burn for up to four hours after the activity has stopped.

The explanation: Legs contain the vast bulk of muscle in
the human, and so the most energy is spent in vigorously exer-
cising them. Now add to the legs, the next-largest groups—
shoulders, chest, and arm muscles. Get them all working
simultaneously and you have the highest calorie-burner of all,
cross-country skiing. It's a little like running on all fours.

Off to the Races

As we explored earlier, cross-country skiing appeals on
many levels. When Bill Koch won the 1982 World Cup, followed not far behind by such bright lights as Tim and Jennifer

Caldwell, Dan Simoneau, and others, it seemed that a topflight ski-racing tradition had finally taken root in America. Subsequent years proved that our early optimism was just that and that the United States is still perhaps five or six generations behind the Europeans—Swedes and Finns most notably.

Yet the Koch years did much for the sport as a sport, the competitive level beyond recreational cruising. Among other things, they raised the consciousness of recreational skiers that, as in running, anyone who can ski can race. And anyone and everyone can ski.

So at one end of the sport is the purely leisure-oriented, relaxed recreationalist. His love is moving slowly through the winter snows and taking his time with his surroundings. That is the skiing most people understood up until the late 1970s when, for a lack of a better term, the Koch years were upon us. Racers, we learned, did not come out of some special School for the Very Hot. Indeed, most fast skiers were skiers who skied a lot, got in shape, and knew the discipline.

Again, as with running, though not everyone is blessed with equal talents, anyone can get in shape and learn to ski well enough to race. And this is the marvelous prospect of citizen ski racing: It is there for anyone who wants it.

Along the Ellis River Trail in the Jackson, New Hampshire, system there is a measured 200-meter section for skiers to time themselves. Tony once waited near the end of that stretch to watch how many skiers were actually working on their times. On this intermediate-level trail, out of a dozen skiers there were ten who ran across the line huffing and puffing and looking at their watches.

Call it the American way, call it competitive instinct, or just allow that there is a natural delight in going fast on skis; the fact is, most skiers would live to race if they could. It is just human nature, once we rise to a certain level of proficiency, to want to test ourselves against a standard. Almost all the major ski-touring centers have citizen races that can be entered for a fee of about a buck. On one level these races are merely fun; on another level they elevate the sport of cross-counrty skiing to an unimaginable height.

Yes, citizen racing has become equivalent to road-running races, and there are several important analogies. Foremost, to

beat a point into the ground, is this: Racing is for everyone and anyone. The hot shots go out and duel for the top one-hundred spots, while the duffer may just like rounding the course to stop at the feed stations. Most skiers are somewhere in the middle. Their contest is against the course, and they're in quest of that old Personal Best.

Races vary from 2-kilometer sprints to 50-kilometer marathons. Nearly all of them are open registration. The United States Ski Association (USSA) has several race series across the country, from 10-kilometer runs to the Great American Ski Chase Series. This is a series of eight marathons, one of which is held at Bretton Woods, New Hampshire, each year. (If marathon distance scares you, there is a one-loop, 25-kilometer version as well.)

One of the really fun races around is the annual Stowe Derby. Here, skiers take off from the top of Mount Mansfield, descend the fire trail for about 2,000 feet (a shallow descent, really), then run the rest of the 10 miles into the town of Stowe, Vermont. Like most citizen races, this is low-key. Many skiers make the run for the wonderful social climate before and during the race and the beer blast afterward.

Aside from ordinary citizen touring, there are all kinds of kinky variations, such as Telemark races, downhill competitions dedicated to that artistic turn invented a century ago by Sondre Nordheim.

Then there is ski orienteering (Ski-O), a race through the wilderness in which skiers must also navigate with a compass and topographical map to find the course. This type of skiing has its roots in ancient military skills. Messengers from the Swedish or Finnish armies would have to find their way across the tundra to deliver crucial information. Thus, performance skiing and woodsmanship were equally tested, for going fast meant little in the wilderness if the messenger didn't know where he was going.

The there's biathlon, triathlon, Nordic combined, and jumping—though these are rather specialized skills for the average weekend skier. Nevertheless, competition abounds everywhere and on every level of seriousness. Nearly every large area has a school with all the information you'll need for the current season in this region. Or, simply ask at the desk of an area where you're skiing. Most likely there will be notices posted about upcoming citizen events.

If improvement is one of your skiing goals, regardless of your current level, there is perhaps no faster path to better performance than learning the disciplines of competitive skiing.

And doesn't that cold drink taste good after a race!

That Question: Wax

To start with an answer, I use both myself. How's that for a hedge?

The question: Who should use a no-wax ski, and who should wax?

I have heard so many sermons on this subject from so many sources that I am often reminded of two political parties in a campaign. Or two fishermen talking about the right fly to use in a stream.

I am also reminded of a heavy-bicycle/light-bicycle analogy. A fellow who runs a nearby bike shop was trying to sell a lightweight French racing bike to a customer who had come into the shop with his sights quite a bit lower. The customer asked what the French racing bike (at nearly twice the money) would do for him that the plainer, cheaper, heavier bike would not do.

"You can't even compare them," said the bike dealer. "It's just another level of the sport. The XYZ bike is more responsive and much much faster. It's another world."

Aside from the fact that the bike salesman had said nothing to really enlighten this customer, he left himself wide open and had utterly no response to the buyer's powerful truth:

"I'm interested in exercise and riding with my family on vacation," said the fellow. "What does it matter how fast I can go?"

If this describes exactly your attitude toward cross-country skiing, as I know it does for many, then go with the no-wax or waxless skis. (Then put a thin protective coat of glider wax on them anyway.)

Here are some other checkpoints for those who should probably go waxless:

. . . If you're an infrequent skier, half a dozen days or less in an average winter.

. . . If it drives you mad to slip backward, even a little bit, going uphill. And you hate to herringbone.

. . . If you live (and ski) in a part of the world where snow conditions vary greatly.

. . . If you hate equipment maintenance of all kinds, and waxing skis strikes you as fussy, scary, and/or stupid.

. . . If the thing you like best about jogging is the simplicity of putting on the shoes and walking out your door.

By these last checkpoints, do not get the idea that waxing is an overly laborious or time-consuming job. I know one certified teacher who goes for an hour's ski run every morning before teaching. His waxing method is to look at the thermometer and then to spend less than five minutes waxing his skis before his run. It is his well-founded belief that if being off by a color really jiggles a skier (unless he is racing), then there's something wrong in his technique.

But back to the waxless skier. As I say, I use both. My waxless skis are mid-thickness Trak Pacers. They are not lightweight, nor are they heavy trucks. The ridge pattern that gives them grip runs over a kick zone of moderate length. In other words, these are mid-everything skis. They'd be right for everyone except the competition skier or that highly experienced runner who likes the feel of flying with wings on his feet.

Much of my casual cross-country skiing begins at my back door. I'll get in an hour or more daily when the snow is good. I ski for a couple of miles through unpathed, hilly woods, ducking through occasional underbrush, then I emerge on a bridle path that circles a horse farm, cross through a broad tree farm beside it, running down through rows of evergreens that make me feel a little like a rat in a maze. Then I pop clear on a lovely eighteen-hole golf course, of which I can digest as much or as little as I have time for before I plunge back into the woods for the trek home.

If the snow is new and deep, I will most likely take the waxless skis. Their size and weight make them easier to break trail with, and I'm not so likely to break one on the jagged woods' floor. Though I'm interested, from an exercise point of view, in keeping a good aerobic pace going, speed per se is not my goal in such conditions. Waxless skis are the choice.

But there is another sort of day. The snow has settled and "set up." In the previous days I have skied tracks into my course, and it may even be a bit firm and fast today. I am not planning any exploratory forays off through unfamiliar woods, and I have a notion to run a few miles—that is, to ski at as fast a pace as I can, to get a nice rhythmic diagonal stride going, to huff and puff a bit.

Or I am at a touring center with trails groomed and track-set. Again, my purpose is to work out, to ski fast and steadily for at least half an hour before a break. In these latter instances, I'll use my pair of skinny, very light and stiff Jarvinen racing skis. Exactly why, when I'm not in a competition of any kind, is hard to say, but it comes down to a matter of feel. The light skinny skis—waxed close to correctly so you're not slipping backward or picking up balls of snow on the kick zone—somehow encourage the skier to go at it a bit more intensely. He leans out over the skis more, throws his hip more into the stride, the pole hand reaching further out and up as he settles into that nice easy rhythm that looks nearly effortless though it produces maximum speed.

Of course, the same pleasing rhythm of the diagonal stride can be performed on waxless skis as well. But the lightweight waxed ski heightens that pleasure to the extreme. The feet feel nearly weightless as the skis glide faster and faster over the snow, and now the skier is into that often-overlooked element in cross-country skiing—speed. And speed on skis reads fun.

This is not to suggest that everyone go buy two pairs of skis simply to explore the extreme range of the sport. But for someone who plans to spend plenty of winter hours working out on skis in the way described above—skiing tracks and predictable terrain—and who finds the prospect of messing around with waxes sort of fun, or at least not disagreeable, then a pair of waxable skis may be in order.

As I said at the outset, this is a rather hedged answer. I own two pairs of skis to prove it.

If you have skied several times on your waxless skis and want to feel the difference, try a demo. Most of the larger touring centers will have most varieties of skis on hand. And if it is clear you are taking a demo run, many rental shops will wax the skis for you and give you a complimentary hour on them.

This may also be a good time for some instruction, for light-weight waxed skis are not quite as forgiving of sloppy technique as are most waxless skis.

Waxing Up

So you've decided to go with a pair of waxable skis: Now what about the waxing?

I don't suppose there is any more-discussed issue in the sport than waxing. It seems to come down to equal parts knowledge, instinct, application technique, and magic.

In the Sierra Nevadas in the 1850s, when mining camps placed heavy wagers of gold dust on miners who would represent them in ski races, the contest often came down to the "doper." He was the ski preparer. In utter secrecy the night before the race, he would mix up his special potion of beeswax, paraffin, and whatever other hopefully charmed ingredients he could think of to apply to the ski bottoms. So much money rode on these races that the doper was regarded as something like the witch doctor who could conjure up just the right spell to make the bottoms of a pair of skis fast.

I am not sure anyone really knows how wax works, though I have listened to many hours of theory. The most cogent primer I recall was that of Jack Turner, a member of the U.S. Ski Team, who at breakfast one morning explained as he diagrammed on his napkin, the following:

Crystals of snow come hard-edged, as in a new snowfall in cold weather, or smooth-sided, as in snow that has thawed and refrozen a few times.

The wax of the day must be sufficiently soft so the crystals of snow will penetrate enough to give the ski its grip but not penetrate so completely that snow will stick to the ski. If the wax you choose for the day is too hard, there will be so little penetration of crystals into the wax that the ski will slip backward when you try to push off on it. Sometimes, good ski technique can get around this tendency, if the problem isn't too extreme. But in the opposite case, the wax is so soft, and the penetration of snow crystals so extreme, the skier will pick up great immobilizing clumps of snow on the kick zone of the ski.

Look elsewhere for a detailed explanation of ski waxing in all its nuances. There are several excellent books on the market, and many of the larger areas will even put on waxing clinics from time to time. Moreover, the more days you ski with people who know what they're about, the quicker you will learn for yourself. And, when all else fails, when you want to know the wax of the day, ask a hotshot. At every touring center I've been to, the morning air is full of discussion about the wax of the day. Listen to this talk. You'll know who the hotshots are right away.

That said, here is the Chamberlain Sometimes Sure-Fire Simpleminded Waxing Style:

Cross-country waxes are color-coded to temperature, and are pretty logical about it. Cold colors—blue and green—are cold-temperature waxes, and warm colors—purples to reds—are for warmer temperatures. So you stick a thermometer in the snow and know just what to do, correct? For real arctic snow, green will be the choice (or maybe special green), blue for merely cold snow, violet for that 32-degree Fahrenheit limbo, and red for thawing snow.

Well, its almost that simple. But not quite.

Despite the temperature, if the snow has thawed and refrozen, its crystal shape will have changed irreversibly. Yesterday's hard-edged new snow, having thawed once or twice, has now lost those hard crystal edges and become old snow with round crystals. Often, the only way to get a grip on such crystals is by using *klister*—gooey stuff that comes in tubes and is color-coded similarly to the hard waxes.

Swix is not the only wax manufacturer around, but it is certainly an identifiable standard. There is a Swix kit that comes complete with all the waxes and klisters you will need. Armed with this kit, a scraper, polishing cork, a rag or paper toweling, and a lightweight propane torch you must answer two questions: What is the temperature of the snow? Are the crystals sharp (newer) or rounded (old)?

If you're a real performance skier, you'll put a grip wax (softer) on the kick zone and a glider (harder) wax on tips and tails. But that's pretty fussy and unnecessary for most users of fiberglass skis. Most of us will put a glider wax—green is my choice—over the entire base of the ski. This seals the bottom, protects it, and is a good base over which to apply the wax of the day. In many cases this base wax is applied just at the be-

ginning of the season. After rubbing on the wax, heat it gently
with the torch, then polish it in to a slick finish. (You may also
make this application with a cool iron, the same as with Alpine
skis, and cork-polish.)

Over this base coat (which you probably have prepared at
home) you'll then make your best guess at the wax of the day.
Even the neophyte, if he has listened to those around him, can
come close. Read the wax tube for temperature range, and look
at your thermometer. If it's fluffy stuff, go green. If it crunches
a bit, blue. If it's good packing for snowballs, purple. If it's
mashed potatoes, red. And if you're very, very lucky, you can
skip the klister; at any rate, start without it.

Also keep in mind:

. . . As a general rule, go with the colder wax. Snow temperature is generally far behind the temperature of a warming day,
and the penalty for being too cold is not so great as the other
way around. Wax too warm, and you'll be planted like a statue.
Also, you can apply warm wax over cold, and klister over hard
wax, but it is almost impossible to do the reverse.

. . . We New Englanders must also watch humidity. On
very humid days, it often pays to wax warmer than temperature indicates.

. . . If you're on prepared tracks, you can wax warmer, get
more kick without paying the price of clinging clumps. But in
unbroken snow, when bushwhacking woods and mountain terrain, wax colder.

You are supposed to do all this waxing in a warm room—either at home or in a waxing room at a touring center—with the
skis at room temperature. But I've seen plenty of top-flight ski
racers sitting on the bumpers of their cars waxing before a race.
Skiers often must wax while underway on the trail, too.

Most fiberglass skis have well-marked kick zones, but a
rule of thumb is to wax from about 1 foot in front of the bind-
ings to 1 foot behind. Rub the wax on side to side in overlap-
ping smears. Then take your cork and rub it over the wax fast
enough to let friction soften it to a nice polish. Repeat this
waxing procedure twice, and you're set for the day, unless you
must rewax for changing conditions.

Suppose you've blown it? You get out on the trail, and

you've got big balls of snow under your feet? And everyone says you can't wax down in color?

Here is where you'll learn fast that, like fly fishing and choosing the right pattern for a salmon stream, no rules are cast in concrete about ski waxing. Get out the scraper and do the best you can to get the wrong wax off, then try to smear the colder wax on. If it doesn't work, daub some cold klister over the whole mess and see if that helps.

There are difficult days for waxing, when the temperature is right around freezing. The best rule I have discovered about these days is to stay on flat terrain. Remember, the worst that can happen is you'll end up walking back to Bloody Mary hour with the skis on your shoulder.

Skating

A "new" technique has developed in the last five years: skating. While Alpine skiers are very familiar with this form of propulsion across flats, the move was not common in cross-country skiing until Bill Koch introduced it in the highest levels of competition in the seventies and went on to win the Nordic World Cup. Swedish great Gunde Svan was next to pick up the technique and develop it until virtually all serious skiers had to skate to keep up.

Both in racing and recreational skiing, skating has been a most controversial development. So horrified were the European traditionalists that they tried to ban skating from top competition and only grudgingly came to accept it. Likewise, ski-touring centers, at first taking a dim view of the technique that carved up their parallel tracks, have been forced to accommodate the growing popularity of skating.

Basically, the skating technique allows the skier to set one ski at a diagonal to the track and thrust off its inside edge, then repeat the move with the alternate ski. What racers found is that skating requires less energy and produces as much as 30 percent more speed than the traditional diagonal stride.

Skating skis are shorter, the poles are longer, and there is no need for grip wax or scales in the kick zone. Some instruction is usually required to pick up the knack. Many areas reviewed in this book have made the transition to skating; some offer separate trails, while others maintain one side of a trail in single trackset and groom the other side for skating.

What to Wear

Dressing for cross-country is a difficult but solvable problem. The key is layers.

Layers of thin clothing can be taken off as the skier heats up, then put back on when he stops pumping and begins to cool down. A typical outfit for a typical day: polypropylene underwear (use nothing else), wind pants below, a light jersey, loose shirt, light sweater, and a nylon shell. Although knickers and Nordic snowflake stockings look natty at the touring center, wear nylon gaiters in the back country. These, in effect, extend the waterproof seal of your ski boots nearly up to the knees.

31

There are all kinds of clothing variations, of course, and if you're really trekking in backcountry, you'll want to pack clothing in which you could survive a winter night.

This goes for the minimal tools, too: screwdriver and duct tape, wax, sunglasses, lip balm, matches, a compass, topographic maps, and any other miscellany you may need on the trail. But keep it simple. Camping stoves and elaborate waxing kits are examples of the unnecessary for me. They don't feel heavy until the tenth mile or so.

CONNECTICUT

N.

Connecticut

Numbers on map refer to towns numbered below

1. East Hartland, *Pine Mountain Ski Touring Center* 36
2. Farmington, *Winding Trails Ski Touring Center* 36
3. Litchfield, *The White Memorial Foundation* 37
4. Norwich, *Quinebaug Valley Ski Touring Center* 38
5. West Suffield, *Cedar Book Farms Cross-Country Ski Center* .. 39

PINE MOUNTAIN SKI TOURING CENTER
Route 179
East Hartland, Connecticut 06027
(203) 653–4279

Hours: 8:30 A.M. to dusk.
Trail System: About 28 kilometers (20 miles).
Trail Difficulty: Easiest, more difficult, most difficult.
Trail Grooming: Groomed and trackset.
Rental Equipment: 200 sets.
Instruction: By appointment. PSIA-certified.
Food Facilities: Snack bar at the center; restaurants nearby.
Lodging: Several inns and motels in the area.
How to Get There: I–91 to Bradley International Airport Exit 40; Route 20 west through East Granby, Granby, and East Hartland, Connecticut; Route 179 south for 2 miles to Pine Mountain.

Even when it rains in much of southern New England, Pine Mountain, the state's second-highest peak at 1,300 feet, usually has a snow covering. The area, located in grand rural snow country about 25 miles northwest of Hartford, features nicely groomed trails through woods and open meadows. While much of this skiing is fast and flat, there are some jerky twisting trails that challenge your skiing skills as well. The center has a full complement of rentals and retail gear, and lunch tables and booths around a huge wood stove. Several motels and inns can be found nearby, including the famous Yankee Peddler Inn and The Old Riverton Inn.

WINDING TRAILS SKI TOURING CENTER
Off Route 4
Farmington, Connecticut 06032
(203) 677–8458

Hours: 9 A.M. to 4:30 P.M.
Trail System: 26 kilometers (about 15 miles).
Trail Difficulty: Easiest, more difficult.

Trail Grooming: Machine groomed (about 8 percent) with the rest skier-tracked.
Rental Equipment: About 200 sets
Instruction: Group and private.
Food Facilities: Snack bar.
Lodging: Several inns and motels in the area.
How to Get There: I-84 to Exit 39, then 1 mile west of Farmington Center to the Winding Trails Farm.

Winding Trails is a 400-acre touring center set in the picturesque hills of Connecticut countryside. The entire trail system—a relatively gentle series of loops over open pasture and wooded roads—is groomed carefully and trackset for smooth, fast skiing. This is an excellent course for the runners of the sport. The center itself has a well-stocked rental shop and places heavy emphasis on its instructional program. Winding Trails is open December through March, during which it throws six nightly wine-and-cheese parties after a moonlight ski tour. In mid-January the center stages its annual Citizen's Race.

THE WHITE MEMORIAL FOUNDATION
Route 202; Box 368
Litchfield, Connecticut 06759
(203) 567-0857

Hours: Tuesday through Saturday, 8:30 A.M. to 4:30 P.M.; Sunday, 2 P.M. to 5 P.M.
Trail System: 48 kilometers (30 miles).
Trail Difficulty: Easiest, more difficult, most difficult.
Trail Grooming: None.
Rental Equipment: No.
Instruction: No.
Food Facilities: In Litchfield.
Lodging: Inns and motels in the area.
How to Get There: From Hartford, Route 202 west through Litchfield for 2½ miles to a left turn at the White Memorial sign.

The White Memorial Foundation is a lovely 4,000-acre sanctuary dedicated to conservation, education, recreation, and nature research. The terrain, with its crisscrossing carriage roads and trails, is still in its uninterrupted natural state; no motor vehicles are allowed anywhere on the property. The skiing is of the primitive, bushwhacking variety, though tracks are generally cut by previous skiers. The countryside is not especially challenging, except to runners, though one or two real twisters can be found if one really wants to find them. The trail loops roll through woods down to the shores of Bantam Lake. There is no trail fee here, though maps may be purchased at the museum for about $1. A warming-waxing-picnicking facility is also available.

QUINEBAUG VALLEY SKI TOURING CENTER
Roosevelt Avenue, Box 29
Norwich, Connecticut 06360
(203) 886–2284

Hours: 9 A.M. to 4 P.M.
Trail System: 11 kilometers (about 7 miles).
Trail Difficulty: Easiest, more difficult, most difficult.
Trail Grooming: Packed but not trackset.
Rental Equipment: 100 sets.
Instruction: PSIA-certified instructor on weekends.
Food Facilities: Snack bar at the center.
Lodging: Hotels, inns, and motels within 3 miles.
How to Get There: Connecticut Turnpike to Route 12 in Norwich. Follow signs.

This active dairy farm features that most pleasant sort of open-field skiing that lets the inexperienced skier practice in a low-stress environment but also allows runners to really work out over tracks well set by previous skiers. From the open fields—cow pastures—skiers can access the nearby woodlands that glance in and out of open pastures. This is fine touring when the snow is available. Norwich is a good-sized town just 3 miles from the touring center and has an entire range of rentals, retail, food, and lodging.

CEDAR BROOK FARMS CROSS-COUNTRY SKI CENTER
1481 Ratley Road
West Suffield, Connecticut 06093
(203) 668–5026

Hours: 9 A.M. to dusk.
Trail System: 10 kilometers (6.2 miles).
Trail Difficulty: Easiest, more difficult.
Trail Grooming: Groomed and trackset daily.
Rental Equipment: More than 100 sets.
Instruction: Yes.
Food Facilities: Small snack bar for soups and sandwiches.
Lodging: In the area, within 8 miles.
How to Get There: Massachusetts Turnpike to I–91 South to
   Route 57. Take Route 57 through Feeding Hills to South-
   west Street, which changes its name to Ratley Road as you
   enter Connecticut.

When the snow is right, this 200-acre touring center offers all
the delights of skiing on a real working New England farm with
pastureland, woods, ponds, and streams well within the reach
of all skiers. Animals (safely confined) watch as you pass
through the pasture. From this open skiing, the trails course
through a very pretty woodland area, then bring skiers back
into the pasture. This can be hard-run ski touring or pleasant,
gentle cruising, as you wish. There's a warming hut on the
property as skiers cross over from a loop through Enchanted
Forest and back through Cornstalk Patch and Scarecrow Hill.
Fanciful names, delightful skiing.

MASSACHUSETTS

MARTHA'S
VINEYARD

NANTUCKET

N.

93

95

1.

7.
16.
14.

2.

11.

9.

90

91

15.

4.

8. 17.

3.

18.

10.

13.

6.

12.

5.

Massachusetts

Numbers on map refer to towns numbered below.

1. Andover, *Rolling Green Ski Touring Center* 44
2. Carlisle, *Great Brook Farm Ski Touring Center* 44
   North Country Ski Touring Center 45
3. Cummington, *Swift River Inn* 46
4. Granville, *Maple Corner Farm Cross-Country Ski Area* 47
5. Great Barrington, *Butternut Ski Touring* 48
6. Lenox, *Kennedy Park* 49
7. Lincoln, *Lincoln Guide Service* 50
8. New Ashford, *Brodie Mountain Cross-Country Touring* 51
9. Northfield, *Northfield Mountain Ski Touring Center* 52
10. Pittsfield, *Canoe Meadows Wildlife Sanctuary* 53
11. Princeton, *Wachusett Mountain Ski Area* 53
12. South Lee, *Oak n' Spruce Resort* 54
13. Washington, *Bucksteep Manor Cross-Country Ski Center* .. 55
14. Wayland, *Cross-Country Skiing and Snowshoeing in Wayland* 56
15. Westfield, *East Mountain Ski Touring Center* 56
16. Weston, *Weston Ski Track* 58
17. Windsor, *Notchview Reservation* 59
18. Worthington, *Hickory Hill Touring Center* 60

ROLLING GREEN SKI TOURING CENTER
311 Lowell Street
Andover, Massachusetts 01810
(508) 475–4066

Hours: 9 A.M. to 4:30 P.M.; night skiing 6 to 9, Tuesday to Friday.
Trail System: 5 kilometers (about 3 miles).
Trail Difficulty: Easiest, more difficult.
Trail Grooming: As needed.
Rental Equipment: 100 sets.
Instruction: PSIA-certified.
Food Facilities: Trail snacks at the center; also a lounge.
Lodging: Rolling Green Host Hotel.
How to Get There: Route 93 to Massachusetts Exit 47; Sheraton is on the right. Touring center is at the Rolling Green Hotel.

Rolling Green is a convenient touring area near downtown Boston yet has surprisingly pleasant skiing with a nice feel of terrain to it. Not upcountry wilderness skiing to be sure, but a fine place to get in shape for those trips, a good midday workout spot, and some real fun and exercise for city people who have only evening hours for themselves. A full weekend lighted loop lets you take those two-hour vacations that make the next day possible. This is also tied into a major hotel with all the amenities.

GREAT BROOK FARM SKI TOURING CENTER
96 Pleasant Hill Lane
Carlisle, Massachusetts 01741
(508) 369–7486

Hours: 9 A.M. to 4:30 P.M.; Tuesday and Thursday, 9 A.M. to 9 P.M.
Trail System: 15 kilometers (about 9 miles).
Trail Difficulty: Easiest, more difficult, most difficult.
Trail Grooming: Groomed and double trackset.
Rental Equipment: Yes.
Instruction: Certified professional ski school.

44

Food Facilities: Snacks, hot cider, coffee, tea.
Lodging: None.
How to Get There: I–495 to Route 4 in Chelmsford; right on Route 4 and follow to Lowell Road.

Just forty minutes from Boston, Great Brook Farm is a fine and complete daytrip ski center with its 15-kilometer trail system winding over farm meadows, though deep woodlands, and over frozen ponds. Like the Weston Track, Great Brook is one of very few areas that offers snow making over a 1-kilometer loop. Night skiing is also available over a 1.5-kilometer loop.

Great Brook caters to organized race programs and youth groups and puts on a citizen race every Tuesday night. There is an organized Bill Koch League for grade-schoolers.

The area is perfect for Boston-area recreational skiers looking for regular exercise or to get in shape for upcountry.

NORTH COUNTRY SKI TOURING CENTER
Carlisle State Forest, Lowell Road
Carlisle, Massachusetts 01741
(508) 369–7486

Hours: 9 A.M. to 4:30 P.M.; Tuesday and Thursday night skiing until 9 P.M.
Trail System: 18 kilometers (about 10 miles).
Trail Difficulty: Easiest, more difficult.
Trail Grooming: Yes.
Rental Equipment: Yes.
Instruction: PSIA-certified.
Food Facilities: Snack bar at the Hart Barn.
Lodging: Hotels and motels in the region.
How to Get There: I–495 to Route 225 east to Carlisle, then north on Lowell Road.

This is another area with the nicely civilized feel of Boston about it. The touring is excellent, encompassing about 500 acres of terrain from cruising golf-course trails to bushwhacking thicket. Much of the touring is over old roads, so the remaining trails are comfortably wide—just in case you have forgotten what it's like to ski beside your spouse rather than behind. There are Tuesday-night races across a 1.3-kilometer loop of man-made snow. The Hart Barn is the heart of the center. Its wood stoves sear with heat all winter as skiers study their maps, wax their skis, or just rest their weary bones as they sip hot chocolate. Trail snacks, as well as some instruction, are available from the center.

SWIFT RIVER INN
South Street, RR 1, Box 234
Cummington, Massachusetts 01026
(413) 634–5751

Hours: 9 A.M. to 5 P.M.; Thursday through Saturday evenings, 6:30 to 9:30 P.M.

Trail System: 20 kilometers (about 13 miles with 1.5 kilometers (about 1 mile) lighted for night skiing.

Trail Difficulty: Easiest, more difficult, most difficult.

Trail Grooming: As needed. Groomed and tracked with some skating.

Rental Equipment: Yes.

Instruction: PSIA-certified school.

Food Facilities: Restaurant at resort.

Lodging: Inn offers 21 rooms in turn-of-the-century style.

How to Get There: Route 91 north to Northampton; Route 9 west to Cummington (26 miles); turn right into town and follow signs.

Swift River, at 1,250 feet in the Berkshire uplands, is the largest and among the most popular ski-touring areas in southern New England. With good elevation despite the southerly location, the skiing usually remains long into the spring.

The well-marked and well-groomed trail system is spread out over 560 acres of rolling foothills that take skiers through the hardwood forests of the wild turkey and over dazzling white meadowland. The trail difficulty is geared toward novice and intermediate skiers with a nice, leisurely "low-stress" feel about the place.

The accommodations include a wonderfully big restaurant and a well-appointed Nordic retail store.

MAPLE CORNER FARM CROSS-COUNTRY SKI CENTER
Beech Hill Road
Granville, Massachusetts 01034
(413) 357–8829

Hours: 9 A.M. to 5 P.M.
Trail System: More than 20 kilometers (about 12 miles) of marked trails; 15 kilometers groomed; access to a 500-acre tract of wilderness skiing.
Trail Difficulty: Easiest, more difficult, most difficult.
Trail Grooming: Groomed and trackset.
Rental Equipment: Yes.
Instruction: Yes.
Food Facilities: Snack bar at the area and a skiers' lounge with open fireplace.
Lodging: Available in the area. Call the main number at the farm for listings.
How to Get There: From the Springfield area follow Route 20 west to Route 23 to Blandford. Stay on route 23 through Blandford Center and down the hill to Beech Hill Road on the left. Follow Beech Hill past the Granville town line. The ski center is ½ mile into Granville, on the left.

Maple Corner Farm Cross-Country Ski Center is located in the Berkshire foothills near the historic General Knox Trail. The ski area is an authentic family farm that has been in continuous operation since 1840. Once a working dairy and beef operation, the farm now raises hay and makes maple syrup and other maple products; visitors can watch the maple sap boiling in the sugar house.

The trails lead skiers through gentle rolling pastures and large meadows, along mountain streams and beaver ponds. One trail runs through the current sugar bush, which includes old sugaring sites of bygone years, then into the hemlock forest beyond. This is one of the lovelier offerings in the Berkshires, and the trails are wonderfully groomed for serious running, if that is your preference. Wilderness skiers have a virtually infinite area of open meadows and woodlands for simple meandering. Sandwiches, homemade soups, hot chocolate, and cider are served around the open fireplace after the day's skiing.

47

BUTTERNUT SKI TOURING
Route 23 (Butternut Ski Area Access Road)
Great Barrington, Massachusetts 01230
(413) 528-0610

Hours: 9 A.M. to 4 P.M. Thursday through Sunday and school vacation weeks.
Trail System: 7 kilometers (about 4½ miles) of tracks, plus open field skiing; no skating.
Trail Difficulty: Easiest, more difficult.
Trail Grooming: Daily.
Rental Equipment: 100 sets.
Instruction: PSIA-certified; group and private lessons.
Food Facilities: Cafeteria at the Butternut Ski Area.
Lodging: Inns, motels, and guest houses in the area.
How to Get There: I-90 to Exit 2 at Lee, Massachusetts; Route 102 west to Route 7 south to Route 23, then east to Butternut.

Like many touring areas associated with established downhill areas, Butternut Ski Touring shares the benefits of the Alpine accommodations (including the nursery for three- to six-year olds), and naturally lures the skinny skiers onto the Alpine slopes to take a shot at some Telemarking. Whether there is any truth to the old chestnut, "If you can walk, you can cross-country ski," it definitely does not apply to Telemark turning on downhill slopes. Butternut, however, is an excellent place to get lessons for this graceful move. The area has an excellent ski school that can take you to the downhill slopes for lessons.

Spreading out from the warming hut beside a pretty pond, the touring area is a pristine piece of the Berkshire countryside whose 7 miles of gentle, well-groomed trails are near a 45-kilometer trail system in Beartown State Forest; the touring center has maps of this system.

KENNEDY PARK
Lenox, Massachusetts 01240
(413) 637–3010

Hours: 7 A.M. to 4 P.M.
Trail System: None; 600-acre park.
Trail Difficulty: Easiest, more difficult.
Trail Grooming: No.
Rental Equipment: At a nearby ski shop. Call for details.
Instruction: No.
Food Facilities: In the Lenox area.
Lodging: In the area.
How to Get There: Take Massachusetts Turnpike to Exit 2;
    west on Route 7 then south to the park in Lenox.

Kennedy Park is an open 600-acre recreation area used year-round for a variety of sports. There is some gladed and wooded terrain around the park, and the many skiers who use the land make good tracks for those who do not like breaking trail. While there are no facilities at the park itself, this Berkshire town offers all services, from food to rentals and retail facilities.

LINCOLN GUIDE SERVICE
Lincoln Road
Lincoln, Massachusetts 01773
(617) 259–9204
Hours: Monday through Wednesday 9 A.M. to 6 P.M.; Thursday and Friday 9 A.M. to 8 P.M.; Saturday and Sunday 9 A.M. to 5 P.M.
Trail System: 20 kilometers (about 13 miles).
Trail Difficulty: Easiest, more difficult.
Trail Grooming: None.
Rental Equipment: 200 sets.
Instruction: PSIA-certified.
Food Facilities: The nearest of three restaurants is within 50 yards of the skiing; lunches and deli counter at area.
Lodging: Motels in the area.
How to Get There: I–95 to Exit 28 (Trapelo Road); west for 2 miles; left at the Lincoln Street stop sign, then 1 mile to the center.

Lincoln Guide Service is partly a retail operation that accesses town-owned conservation land and partly a dream of Mike Farny to put together a significant touring area especially convenient to people from greater Boston. The open conservation land begins at the center's back door, and a rolling, well-groomed trail system branches out through the country where Henry David Thoreau hiked and observed nature. One of the trails, in fact, leads skiers along ponds of the Sudbury River to Thoreau's beloved Walden Pond in Concord, while other trails mix challenge with relaxing cruises. All trails are well marked, and the center is well stocked with rental and retail goods.

BRODIE MOUNTAIN CROSS-COUNTRY TOURING
Route 7
New Ashford, Massachusetts 01237
(413) 443–4752

Hours: 9 A.M. to 5 P.M.
Trail System: 25 kilometers (about 16 miles).
Trail Difficulty: Easiest, more difficult, most difficult.
Trail Grooming: Yes, trackset with two flat areas; skating lanes.
Rental Equipment: Yes.
Instruction: Yes.
Food Facilities: The Blarney Room in the main lodge serves lunch and dinner.
Lodging: Hotel at the ski area, and several facilities nearby.
How to Get There: Route 2 to Route 7; north for 9 miles beyond Pittsfield. Midway between Pittsfield and Williamstown on Route 7.

This popular Berkshire-region Alpine area incorporates the advantages of snow-making and base-lodge facilities into its Nordic facility. The trail system combines about 25 kilometers of wide, groomed and trackset trails with another 40 kilometers of wilderness touring, then limitless bushwhacking out in the Mount Greylock Reservation. The skiing has good variety, from rolling pastureland and open fields, to heart-pumping hills and closed, wooded roads that meander through these Berkshire foothills and past some most unusual rock formations. This is a land fecund with wildlife of all kinds. The groomed trail system was designed by former Olympic skier Bud Fischer and is used for training by the Williams College Ski Team. Tennis, racketball, and sauna are available, and several races are staged here throughout the season.

NORTHFIELD MOUNTAIN SKI TOURING CENTER
Route 63
Northfield, Massachusetts 01360
(413) 659-3713

Hours: 9 A.M. to 5 P.M.
Trail System: 40 kilometers (25 miles).
Trail Difficulty: Easiest, more difficult, most difficult.
Trail Grooming: Daily.
Rental Equipment: Yes.
Instruction: PSIA-certified.
Food Facilities: Chocolate Pot snack area; outdoor barbecue-pit food service at base lodge; both open on weekends and holidays only.
Lodging: Several motels and inns within 5 miles of the center.
How to Get There: I-91 to Exit 27; Route 2 east to Route 63 north; 2 miles to the center.

More than 40 kilometers of double tracks set daily over wide trails groomed with Alpine equipment, an active racing program, and a lineup of instructors who teach some 5,000 skiers annually make Northfield one of the largest learning centers in southern New England. The area pioneered the concept of grooming with Alpine rollers and prides itself on creating a ski surface just a little bigger and better than average.

In addition to recreational family touring, Northfield also takes pride in its Fast-Track Ski Camp for would-be racers who want to learn the sport from the likes of former U.S. Ski Team Olympian Tim Caldwell. Hank Lange and John Tidd are also PSIA instructors.

Three well-traveled trail systems converge at The Chocolate Pot, where skiers warm themselves in front of a big fire and sip hot chocolate and soup. Other snacks are available from an outdoor barbecue pit. During the week Northfield Mountain offers instruction and rentals for elementary-school-agers. Six miles of trails are reserved for snowshoers.

CANOE MEADOWS WILDLIFE SANCTUARY
Holmes Road
Pittsfield, Massachusetts 01201
(413) 637–0320

Hours: 9 A.M. to 4 P.M., weekends only.
Trail System: 5 kilometers (about 3 miles).
Trail Difficulty: Easiest.
Trail Grooming: No.
Rental Equipment: None at facility. Ski shop nearby, in Lenox.
Instruction: Saturday clinics by appointment.
Food Facilities: None at ski area, but restaurants nearby.
Lodging: Motels and inns in area.
How to Get There: Massachusetts Turnpike to Exit 2 at Lee;
    Route 7 to Holmes Road. Turn right and drive for 2 miles
    to entrance of Canoe Meadows Wildlife Sanctuary.

Canoe Meadows is a Massachusetts Audubon Society sanctuary comprised of 260 wooded acres bordered by the Housatonic River. It is not so much a ski facility as simply a lovely piece of wild land open for weekend ski touring. There are wildlife tours of the property by appointment. Outhouses are available on the site.

WACHUSETT MOUNTAIN SKI AREA
Mountain Road
Princeton, Massachusetts 01541
(508) 464–2788

Hours: Weekdays 9 A.M. to dusk; Saturday, Sunday, and holidays, 8 A.M. to dusk.
Trail System: 19 kilometers (about 11 miles).
Trail Difficulty: Easiest, more difficult, most difficult.
Trail Grooming: Groomed and trackset, as needed.
Rental Equipment: Yes.
Instruction: 10:30 A.M. to 1 P.M., or by appointment. Telemark.
    PSIA instructors.
Food Facilities: Full cafeteria with lounge and ice-cream shop.

Lodging: Several hotels and motels within a fifteen-minute drive. *How to Get There:* Route 2 west to Route 140 south. The area is 3½ miles from the exit.

Close to Boston, Wachusett is another of those touring areas that brings the amenities of the downhill area and the challenge to cross-country skiers to try their hand—and feet—at Telemarking down Alpine slopes. Instruction is necessary for this, and it is available. The area's 19 kilometers of groomed and trackset trails wind over the top of Wachusettt's 2,000-foot elevation and offer skiers a nice view of what Indians named "the great hill." The cross-country trails are wide and well maintained, and the terrain has some spicy variety for all levels of skier. Maps, rentals, instruction, and full base-lodge facilities.

OAK n' SPRUCE RESORT
South Lee, Massachusetts 01260
(413) 243-3500

Hours: Dawn to dusk.
Trail System: 10 mile loop; novice area; 50 kilometers (about 30 miles) of trails in the adjoining state forest, open to the public.
Trail Difficulty: Easiest, more difficult.
Trail Grooming: On the 2-mile novice loop.
Rental Equipment: 100 sets.
Instruction: Yes.
Food Facilities: Continental-style restaurant; hot drinks and snacks at center.
Lodging: 150 units (condos and hotel rooms) at the resort.
How to Get There: Massachusetts Turnpike to Exit 2 in Lee; Route 102 west to Oak n' Spruce.

This touring center has 300 acres of open fields and a groomed, trackset 2-mile loop. But after warming up here, skiers plunge into the 12,000-acre Beartown State Forest and follow the unplowed country roads, forest trails, and open-meadow touring. This is the pristine land of the whitetailed deer and wild turkey.

For beginners or serious touring skiers, Oak n' Spruce accommodates all levels. Aside from planned group activities—snowshoeing, skating, and tobogganing—the area has plenty of health club-pool-sauna-Jacuzzi-cocktail lounge activity for the indoor sports enthusiast.

BUCKSTEEP MANOR CROSS-COUNTRY SKI CENTER
Washington Mountain Road
Washington, Massachusetts 01223
(413) 623-5535

Hours: 8 A.M. to 4:30 P.M.
Trail System: 25 kilometers (about 16 miles).
Trail Difficulty: Easiest, more difficult, most difficult.
Trail Grooming: Machine trackset, as needed; some skating lanes.
Rental Equipment: 100 sets; retail shop.
Instruction: Private and group, by appointment.
Food Facilities: Manor Kitchen Restaurant on premises serves meals weekends and holidays. Skier Sunday Brunch special; lunch all week.
Lodging: Manor Inn, call (413) 623-5535.
How to Get There: I-90 to Exit 2 at Lee; Route 20 east, then Route 8 north to Washington.

High atop the Berkshire Hills between October and Washington peaks, Bucksteep Manor's 1,900-foot elevation ensures one of the longest ski seasons in the region. The nicely groomed trails wind through snow-covered fir thickets, stream beds, and bogs, and across pristine white meadows that overlook mountain valleys. Skiers can also incorporate on their tour the trail system of nearby October Mountain.

As picturesque as the land is the Manor Inn itself, a Victorian estate that serves fine homemade food in front of a big wood fire. Here are nightly entertainment and moonlight tours. Bucksteep offers citizen racing and guided tours of the Appalachian Trail. Sleigh rides in the state forest are also offered.

CROSS-COUNTRY SKIING AND SNOWSHOEING IN WAYLAND
Conservation Commission
Wayland, Massachusetts 01778
(508) 358–7701 weekdays

How to Get There: I–95 to Route 20 to Wayland.

Although Wayland is not the only community to open large tracts of public land to skiing and snowshoeing, it is one of the best, certainly considering how close it is to the large metropolitan area of greater Boston. The Conservation Commission makes no special effort to groom or trackset—or even to clear fallen brush from the trails. Yet the woodland trails, which web throughout almost 600 acres of woods and open meadows, are often traced by skiers very soon after a new snowfall. There are four areas: Heard Farm, Cow Common, Upper Mill Brook, and Mainstone Area. Heard Farm is the best skiing area. The parcel consists of a scenic farm with rolling meadows and woods full of wildlife. It is accessible from a parking lot off the end of Heard Road. Cow Common, close to the original Sudbury village, is similar to Heard Farm but somewhat flatter. It has parking off Route 27. Upper Mill Brook is entirely wooded, and the skiing is tougher by far. Mainstone has lots of trails, but the equestrians often ride the snow off them early in the day. The trustees do keep the trails marked and graded—a good thing since there are some really tough descents that one should know about beforehand. They also provide a map of the entire area. Happily, no motorized vehicles are allowed in Wayland's conservation.

EAST MOUNTAIN SKI TOURING CENTER
East Mountain Country Club
East Mountain Road
Westfield, Massachusetts 01085
(413) 568–1539

Hours: Weekends and vacation weeks, 10 A.M. to 4 P.M.
Trail System: 26 kilometers (about 15 miles).
Trail Difficulty: Easiest, more difficult, most difficult.

56

Trail Grooming: Groomed and trackset daily.
Rental Equipment: Yes.
Instruction: Yes.
Food Facilities: Snacks and bar at the center.
Lodging: Motels and inns in the area.
How to Get There: I–90 to West Springfield, Massachusetts;
    Route 20 west; just after the West Springfield-Westfield
    line, turn right onto East Mountain Road.

Located in the vicinity of the fabled trout river (the Westfield
River), this touring center begins with a marked and groomed
trail system webbed over about 800 acres, then pushes out into
the rural environs of these Berkshire foothills and pastures. The
area of wilderness touring is loaded with wildlife from small
birds to wild turkey and deer. The range of skiing is flat to very
hilly and challenging in spots. East Mountain has a serviceable
snack bar, with retail-rental facilities.

WESTON SKI TRACK
At the Leo J. Martin Golf Course
Box 426, Park Road
Weston, Massachusetts
(617) 894-4903

Hours: Monday through Saturday 9 A.M. to 10 P.M.; Sunday 9
   A.M. to 6 P.M.
Trail System: 15 kilometers (about 9 miles).
Trail Difficulty: Easiest, more difficult.
Trail Grooming: Trackset daily; skating lanes.
Rental Equipment: Yes.
Instruction: PSIA-certified.
Food Facilities: Cafe and snack bar on premises.
Lodging: Many hotels and motels in the area.
How to Get There: I–90 to Exit 15, onto I–95 to exit 25; north
   to Route 30, then west to a left turn onto Park Road and to
   Weston Ski Track.

As cross-country skiing caught on among Bostonians during
the last two decades, a need arose for local areas near the city.
Mike Farny and The Lincoln Guide Service, given a shove by
M. R. Montgomery of the *Boston Globe,* opened the Weston
Track on a popular MDC golf course. Since those origins in the
early 1970s, the area has grown as a place to work out, to get
excellent lessons, and to practice for trips upcountry.
    And lest ye think Weston sounds rather small and insignifi-
cant, you'll encounter some of the serious folks in the sport
here, wearing their one-piece body suits and zinging around the
loops at 15 miles an hour. Here high school and college teams
work out over the carefully groomed tracks. The addition of
snow making makes it possible to ski here even when there's
no snow in the flatlands. After a workout, skiers relax in the
Langlaufer Cafe, whose name translates: "Cross-country skiers
live longer." There are showers, lockers, waxing areas, and a
full retail shop. It goes without saying that there are plenty of
citizen races at the track, as well as clinics on everything from
waxing to skating technique.

NOTCHVIEW RESERVATION
Route 9
Windsor, Massachusetts 01262
(413) 684-0148

Hours: Dawn to dusk from December 1 through March 1.
Trail System: 25 kilometers (about 16 miles); 3,000-acre reservation.
Trail Difficulty: Easiest, more difficult, and most difficult.
Trail Grooming: On the main trail only.
Rental Equipment: No.
Instruction: None.
Food Facilities: Picnic room, and several restaurants within 5 miles.
Lodging: Several motels and inns within 5 miles in Windsor and Stockbridge.
How to Get There: Massachusetts Turnpike to Lee; Route 7 north to Pittsfield, Massachusetts; then Route 9 east for about 14 miles to Notchview.

Many knowledgeable cross-country aficionados consider Notchview one of the best wilderness ski areas in the Berkshires, with its 25-kilometer spider web of trails for every level of skiing challenge. Main loops plunge along through this spruce forest so appreciated by small game, deer, and a growing flock of wild turkeys. Ancient stone walls and cellar holes poignantly bespeak a rugged farming history. Part of the Hoosac Range, Notchview Reservation has a system of trails running over old fire and logging roads, with clear difficulty-level signs at each intersection, all at a mile-high elevation.

The main loop, Circuit Trail, leads to a pasture with a sudden vista of the notch, cut by Shaw Brook, a tributary of the Westfield River. It is this view that gives the area its name. A most challenging trail is a steep climb up Judges Hill, rising to 2,300 feet, the highest point in Windsor. The snow comes early here and hangs in late because of the spruce shade. Budds Visitors Center is on the premises with rest rooms, a picnic room with a big fireplace, and a waxing room. Notchview is one of sixty-nine properties owned by the Trustees of Reservations, a private, nonprofit organization founded in 1891 to preserve beautiful and historic places in Massachusetts.

HICKORY HILL TOURING CENTER
Box 39
Buffington Hill Road
Worthington, Massachusetts 01098
(413) 238-5813

Hours: 9 A.M. to dusk.
Trail System: 25 kilometers (about 15 miles).
Trail Difficulty: Easiest, more difficult, most difficult.
Trail Grooming: Machine double trackset.
Rental Equipment: 250 sets.
Instruction: Yes.
Food Facilities: Food service in the barn on weekends; cocktails and meals.
Lodging: Inns and motels in the area within 20 miles; bed-and-breakfast nearby.
How to Get There: I-91 to Northampton; Route 9 northwest to Route 143; west on Route 112 and Worthington, then right onto Buffington Hill Road.

With an expanded trail system, good elevation (1,800 feet) to ensure long seasons, and improvements each year, Hickory Hill is developing as a popular ski center in the Berkshires.

The 25 kilometers of groomed, trackset, and well-marked trails are spread out over 700 acres of old New England farm country and adjoining hardwood forests. The rolling meadowland is interlaced with old colonial stone walls, and in spots skiers are treated to lovely overlooks of 40 miles and more out toward New York State. Hickory Hill offers a special package for beginners. Maps and trail guides are available. The barn serves beverages, baked goods, and a soup du jour in front of a constantly roaring fireplace. There is a fulsome schedule of moonlight and maple-sugar tours, as well as an old-fashioned pig roast in mid-season. The high elevation usually ensures excellent snow cover.

VERMONT

17.

26.

16.

18.

10.

11.

42.

14.

91

7.

40.

34.

2.

15.

27.

22.

36.

37.

5.

25.

89

12.

32.

31.

3.

33.

9.

43.

30.

19.

6.

N.

23.

20.

8.

29.

21.

24.

13.

1.

35.

39.

38.

28.

41.

4.

Vermont

Numbers on map refer to towns numbered below.

1. Arlington, *The West Mountain Inn* 64
2. Bolton Valley, *Bolton Valley Cross Country Center* 65
3. Brandon, *Churchill House Inn and Ski Touring Center* 66
4. Brattleboro, *Brattleboro Outing Club Ski Hut* 67
5. Brookfield, *Green Trails Inn & Ski Touring Center* 67
6. Brownsville, *Ascutney Mountain Resort Touring Center* 68
7. Burlington, *The Catamount Trail Association* 69
8. Chester, *Ski Tours of Vermont* 70
   Tater Hill Cross-Country Ski Center 71
9. Chittenden, *Mountain Top Ski Touring Center* 72
10. Craftsbury Common, *Craftsbury Nordic Ski Center* 73
11. East Burke, *Burke Mountain Ski Touring Center* 74
12. Goshen, *Blueberry Hill* 75
13. Grafton, *Grafton Ponds Cross-Country Ski Center* 76
14. Greensboro, *Highland Lodge* 77
15. Huntington, *Camel's Hump Nordic Ski Center* 78
16. Irasburg, *Heermansmith Farm* 79
17. Jay, *Jay Peak Ski Area* 80
18. Jeffersonville, *Red Fox Ski Touring Center* 81
    Sterling Ridge Inn 82
19. Killington, *Mountain Meadows Ski Touring Center* 83
20. Landgrove, *Nordic Inn Ski Touring Center* 84
21. Londonderry, *Viking Ski Touring Centre* 85
22. Lower Waterford, *Rabbit Hill Inn* 85
23. Ludlow, *Fox Run Resort* 86
24. Manchester, *Birch Hill Inn* 87
    Hildene Ski Touring Center 88
25. Middlebury, *Carrol and Jane Rikert Ski Touring Center* 89
26. Montgomery Center, *Alpine Haven* 89
    Hazen's Notch Ski Touring Center 91
    Vermont Voyager Expeditions 92
27. Montpelier, *The Montpelier Elks Ski Touring Center* 92
28. Old Bennington, *Prospect Mountain Ski Touring Center* 93
29. Peru, *Wild Wings Ski Touring Center* 94
30. Quechee, *Wilderness Trails and Nordic Ski School* 94
31. Randolph, *Green Mountain Touring Center* 95
32. Rochester, *Nordic Adventures* 96
33. Stockbridge, *Trail Head Ski Touring Center* 97
34. Stowe, *Edson Hill Manor* 98
    Mt. Mansfield Ski Touring Center 99
    Topnotch Touring Center 100
    Trapp Family Lodge 102
35. Stratton Mountain, *Stratton Mountain Cross-Country Center* 103
36. Waitsfield, *Tucker Hill Ski Touring Center* 104
37. Warren, *Ole's Cross Country* 105
    Sugarbush Inn/Rossignol Ski Touring Center 106
38. West Dover, *Timber Creek Ski Touring Center* 107
39. West Townshend, *Windham Hill Inn & Touring Center* 107
40. Williston, *Catamount Family Center* 108
41. Wilmington, *Hermitage Cross-Country Touring Center* 109
    Inn at Quail Run 110
    Sitzmark Lodge 111
    The White House Touring Center 112
42. Wolcott, *Hilltop Cross-Country Center* 113
43. Woodstock, *Woodstock Ski Tour Center* 114

THE WEST MOUNTAIN INN
Route 313, River Road
Arlington, Vermont 05250
(802) 375–6516

Hours: Daylight.
Trail System: 9 kilometers (about 5 miles).
Trail Difficulty: Easiest, more difficult, most difficult.
Trail Grooming: None; wilderness trails.
Rental Equipment: None.
Instruction: None.
Food Facilities: Breakfast, 8 A.M. to 10 A.M.; dinner 7 P.M., by reservation only.
Lodging: Rooms at the inn.
How to Get There: Route I–91 to Brattleboro, Vermont; Route 9 west to Bennington; Route 7 north to Arlington, then Route 313 west to West Mountain Road, and up the hill.

This wilderness area contains the best sort of Vermont inn—hidden in the splendid intimate surroundings of the Batten Kill River woodlands. From the door of the inn skiers look over the famous Batten Kill with its trout-fishing lore, then begin to work off breakfast, first on the easy flats, then on the seemingly endless ruggedness of the old logging trails. Some of these trails can get woolly and steep, but they are quite wide. Nearer the inn is a wonderful all-purpose hill for Telemark practice or moonlight tobogganing.

At night in front of the inn's huge fireplace, you'll be served as fine cuisine as there is in Vermont, starting with hot drinks and cocktails and followed by an artistic meal and after-dinner activity around the piano. There are thirteen rooms, cottages, and a two-bedroom housekeeping apartment as well.

BOLTON VALLEY CROSS COUNTRY CENTER
Bolton Valley Ski Resort
Bolton, Vermont 05477
(802) 434–2131

Hours: 9 A.M. to 4 P.M.
Trail System: More than 100 kilometers (about 60 miles).
Trail Difficulty: Easiest, more difficult, most difficult.
Trail Grooming: 10 kilometers rolled and trackset; 20 kilometers rolled; remainder, wilderness skiing.
Rental Equipment: Yes.
Instruction: Beginning group to private Telemark.
Food Facilities: Eight separate dining experiences.
Lodging: Bolton Valley Lodge has an eighty-five-bed capacity; other motels and inns in the area.
How to Get There: I–95 to I–89 to Exit 10; Route 2 and Bolton access road to the ski area.

Bolton Valley's gentle Alpine slopes work to the ski tourer's advantage. The area has a very well developed Nordic trail system set into the 2,100-foot elevation, and that means snow—lots of it—well into April most years. But take advantage of Bolton's downhill capability, and you will become an expert Telemarker as well. Skiers begin with the Sitzmark Trail, graduate to the intermediate Telemark trail, then try Cliffhanger, where the trail system works into the Trapp Family Lodge and Mt. Mansfield—a trek for experts. Skiers taking this route or any other may take the group lessons available at Bolton Valley beginning at 10 A.M. Aside from a full-complement retail and rental shop, Bolton Valley has all the amenities of a major downhill ski area, and cross-country tourers are welcome as well.

CHURCHILL HOUSE INN AND SKI TOURING CENTER
Route 73
Brandon, Vermont 05733
(802) 247-3300

Hours: 10 A.M. to 4 P.M.
Trail System: 40 kilometers (25 miles).
Trail Difficulty: Easiest, more difficult, most difficult.
Trail Grooming: 20 kilometers groomed and trackset daily.
Rental Equipment: No.
Instruction: Yes.
Food Facilities: Dining for guests; other restaurants within 5 miles.
Lodging: Nine rooms at the inn with many hotels and motels in the area.
How to Get There: I–91 to I–89 west; to exit 3; west on Route 107 to 100 north to Route 73 west; 13 miles on 73 west.

Churchill House is part of a three-lodge, four-day inn-to-inn trip from north to south that lets skiers get some real miles under the boards traveling from Bristol to Chittenden. Churchill is a stout, three-story farmhouse of the Civil War period and preserves the century-old feel inside and out. The trail system begins with groomed and trackset loops of flattish terrain near the inn, then flowers out into some rugged wilderness challenge. Along several of the trail systems, skiers get sudden vistas of the Adirondacks. The system winds into the Green Mountain National Forest and its nearly limitless skiing. Back at the inn, with its full fare of cocktails and gourmet dining, skiers find rentals and retail available, guided tours, and organized events. In the waxing hut, hot soup and bread are always available to see one through to the inn's sumptuous meals.

BRATTLEBORO OUTING CLUB SKI HUT
Box 335, Upper Drummerston Road
Brattleboro, Vermont 05301
(802) 254-4081 or (802) 254-4712

Hours: 9 A.M. to 4 P.M.
Trail System: 15 kilometers (about 9 miles).
Trail Difficulty: Easiest, more difficult.
Trail Grooming: All trails packed for skating and trackset.
Rental Equipment: Yes.
Instruction: By appointment.
Food Facilities: 2 miles away in Brattleboro.
Lodging: In Brattleboro.
How to Get There: I-93 to Brattleboro to second exit; Route 30 to Upper Dummerston Road to the Outing Club.

This wide-open ski area is spread out across a 9-hole golf course and the nearby woodlands. The trails are groomed and used often by the more athletic of the cross-country fraternity. Some trails cross bridges and skirt ponds; others are flat runners along the fairways. The system is anchored by a center with ski shop, warming hut, rentals, and snacks. Skiers here can also sign up for moonlight excursions.

GREEN TRAILS INN & SKI TOURING CENTER
Pond Village
Brookfield, Vermont 05036
(802) 276-3412 or (800) 243-3412

Hours: 9 A.M. to 5 P.M.
Trail System: 36 kilometers (about 23 miles).
Trail Difficulty: Easiest, more difficult, most difficult.
Trail Grooming: Machine groomed and trackset.
Rental Equipment: Yes.
Instruction: PSIA-certified instructors by appointment at the inn.
Food Facilities: Breakfast and dinner at the center's restaurant; lunches available to skiers.
Lodging: Fifteen rooms at the inn.

How to Get There: I–91 to I–89, northeast to Vermont Exit 4; Route 66 east to Randolph Center, then north for 7½ miles to Brookfield. Signs to the center.

Green Trails Inn & Ski Touring Center is an area that keeps evolving around what was once nineteenth-century farmland in the historic village of Brookfield, Vermont. Encompassing a restored farmhouse and two other residences, the center offers fifteen nice rooms with plenty of Victorian and early American flavor. The ski-trail system keeps expanding over the rolling pastureland, frozen lakes, and hills of the region; one trail takes skiers across the famed floating bridge over a narrow pond. Skating, snowshoeing, and sleigh rides complete this winter postcard scene. The trail system itself incorporates other nearby trail systems for plenty of skiing—including the Allis State Park on 400 acres of groomed and wilderness trails. The center has complete rental and retail offerings, and the food is homemade and delicious.

ASCUTNEY MOUNTAIN RESORT TOURING CENTER
Route 44
Brownsville, Vermont 05037
(802) 484–7711 or 800–243–0011

Hours: Saturday, Sunday, all holidays, and vacation weeks, 8:30 A.M. to 4 P.M.
Trail System: 32 kilometers (20 miles).
Trail Difficulty: Easiest, more difficult, most difficult.
Trail Grooming: Daily.
Rental Equipment: Yes.
Instruction: Yes.
Food Facilities: Cafeteria at the Ascutney Alpine area nearby.
Lodging: Inns and motels in the area.
How to Get There: I–91 to Route 44 in Vermont; west to the touring center.

This broad plateau looks down on the white-steepled village of Brownsville and beyond to the pretty white swaths of the Ascutney Alpine area, a tall tower of a peak. For tourers, the surroundings are lumpy and very pretty—the essence of Vermont's Green Mountain countryside. The 32 kilometers of trail undulate through this land over pasture, along a stream bed, and through deep fir thickets. Nearly all of it is gentle until you take the guided backcountry tours—including overnight trips by arrangement—at which point the skiing becomes a bit of a challenge. At the warming hut and rental shop, skiers can arrange for lessons.

THE CATAMOUNT TRAIL ASSOCIATION
Box 897
Burlington, Vermont 05402

The core of the Catamount Trail Association (CTA) is a group of fanatic skiers who trekked the length of Vermont in March 1984 and who now dedicate themselves to the proposition that all skiers could and should ski on North America's longest trail—from Massachusetts to Quebec.

Steve Bushey, Paul Jarris, and Ben Rose hatched the idea that by linking the trails of several touring areas together with old roads along the ridge line of the Green Mountains, the entire length of the state can be easily traversed. The route selected is a skiing nirvana: a trail that runs through deep woods and open fields; over long descents down forgotten roads; over clearings with sudden views of mountain and valley; and down into amiable New England villages as you trek along north. The largest part of this "winter-long" trail, as its creators call it, is already accessible to skiers in the form of unplowed roads connected to groomed ski-center trails and other public ways. However, there are several sections that still must be cleared, and Catamount Trail Association members—present and future—are going about the task. Anyone who joins CTA (write at the above address) will be kept informed of developments by newsletter.

With an average elevation of between 1,500 and 2,000 feet, the trail system will have reliable snow cover and will constitute a skiing resource of every level of Nordic aficionado. The trail begins at the White House in Wilmington, Vermont, and roughly parallels Route 100 up to Hermitage, Stratton, Nordic Inn, and the Village Inn outside of Londonderry. The trek then pushes north over the Green Mountains toward Rutland, where it picks up Mountain Meadows near Killington; then Mountain Top, Blueberry Hill, Sugarbush, Tucker Hill, Camel's Hump, and the Trapp Family Lodge at Stowe along with Mansfield. From Mansfield, the tour pushes up on the 10th Army Mountain road to Top Notch, Edson Hill, Craftsbury, Hazen's Notch, and on to its terminus at Jay Peak.

SKI TOURS OF VERMONT
RFD 1
Chester, Vermont 05143
(802) 824–6012

How to Get There: Massachusetts Turnpike to I–91 exit; follow to Route 11 in Vermont.

Rather than a particular destination, Ski Tours of Vermont is a guide and instruction service in the National Forest of Weston and Londonderry, Vermont. Tours access the Great Vermont Ski Trail and offer personalized outfitting and instruction. Treks vary from three to eight days and put together inn-to-inn touring—the ultimate in the trekking end of the sport—at its very best. Aside from encountering a variety of terrain types as you ski through the Green Mountains, you will stay at country inns—from old New England farmhouses to former country gentlemen's estates—and sample all sorts of cuisines, from French, to Swiss, to genuine New England. Meanwhile your luggage is sent along to your next stop. Like most ski-guide services, Ski Tours will match a trip to the skier's ability, experience, and taste. But make plans early.

TATER HILL CROSS-COUNTRY SKI CENTER
Chester, Vermont 05143
(802) 875-2517

Hours: 9:00 A.M. to 4:30 P.M.
Trail System: 40 kilometers (about 25 miles).
Trail Difficulty: Easiest, more difficult, most difficult.
Trail Grooming: Over about 20 kilometers.
Rental Equipment: Yes.
Instruction: Yes.
Food Facilities: On the premises.
Lodging: Within 3 miles.
How to Get There: Follow I-91 to Exit 6; Route 103 north to Chester; then Route 11 west to the center, between Chester and Londonderry.

Tater Hill Center is a good-sized trail system surrounding a 200-year-old farmhouse in central Vermont. It offers good skiing on groomed trails, as well as some real wilderness experience breaking trail as you ski out to the tough Williams River loop. To get your bearings first, the Whitetail and Sweet Potater

71

trails are flat running loops, both of which pass warming shelters along the way. Most trails pass through hardwood forest with some nice views of the rolling Green Mountain foothills. Back at the inn, food and drink are available in the post-Revolutionary flavor of so many Vermont inns. Through the season there are several races organized, along with the annual Scandinavian Night, a moonlight cruise followed by an embarrassment of caloric riches at the smorgasbord table.

MOUNTAIN TOP SKI TOURING CENTER
Chittenden, Vermont 05737
(802) 483–6089

Hours: 9 A.M. to 5 P.M.
Trail System: 110 kilometers (about 70 miles); all but 20 kilometers groomed for skating.
Trail Difficulty: Easiest, more difficult, most difficult.
Trail Grooming: When fully open, 70 kilometers groomed daily. One side double track, one side groomed for skating.
Rental Equipment: 125 sets.
Instruction: PSIA-certified.
Food Facilities: Snack bar at the touring center; full-service restaurant at the Mountain Top Inn.
Lodging: Mountain Top Inn, a full-service hotel with fifty rooms.
How to Get There: I–93 to I–89; take Exit 1 and Route 4 west to Rutland. Follow signs for Mountain Top Ski Touring just past the entrance to Pico Peak.

Just when you think you've seen all of Vermont's country inns and ski-touring areas, there is another inn, another area more beautiful than the last. That's the first impression one gets from Mountain Top, with its enormous trail system that winds out through dazzling white meadows and quiet hardwood forest land. The elevation—2,000 feet—gives Mountain Top excellent capacity to hold snow as well as some stunning panoramic views of the peaks and lakes of the Green Mountain National Forest. In addition, Mountain Top makes its own snow on a 5-kilometer track loop that is a fine warm-up and exercise area for all ability levels.Beyond that, there is skiing over the gently rolling Alpine meadows and spruce forest and then some toe-curling challenge for experts over tough, twisting, choppy trails with steep verticals. The ski season holds well into the spring here.

At day's end, the Ski Shop, a converted horse barn warmed by a big wood stove, has a full complement of retail and rental gear, hot soups, drinks, and snacks. There is also a sun deck for the mild days. Skiers can sign up here for lessons, waxing and racing clinics, seminars, and films. Remember that the area is near two big downhill centers (Pico and Killington), so visitors should seek advance reservations.

CRAFTSBURY NORDIC SKI CENTER
Box 31
Craftsbury Common, Vermont 05827
(802) 586–7767

Hours: 9 A.M. to 5 P.M. (night skiing under the lights).
Trail System: 65 kilometers (about 40 miles).
Trail Difficulty: Easiest, more difficult, most difficult.
Trail Grooming: Daily. Single trackset and skating lanes.
Rental Equipment: Yes.
Instruction: Private and group lessons.
Food Facilities: Buffet-style dining—three meals.
Lodging: Ski dorm, apartments, cottages, and fifty other units
    at the center.
How to Get There: I–89 to Montpelier, Vermont; Route 14 to
    Craftsbury.

Located in one of the wildest stretches of New England—the Northeast Kingdom—Craftsbury's 65 kilometers of trails, including a full skating track, are groomed to a fault and are maintained for racing as well as casual recreational skiing. The trail system winds into others in the region, accessing about 110 kilometers and encompassing the entire town of Craftsbury. Two other fine New England inns are located along the trail system.

With one of the longest seasons in the East—November to April—Craftsbury offers excellent skiing over the whole ability range, from beginners to serious veterans and racers. Children are welcome at all facilities at Craftsbury.

BURKE MOUNTAIN SKI TOURING CENTER
RR1, Box 62A
East Burke, Vermont 05832
(802) 626–8338

Hours: 9 A.M. to sunset.
Trail System: 53 kilometers (about 31 miles).
Trail Difficulty: Easiest, more difficult, most difficult.
Trail Grooming: Yes. One half groomed for skating.
Rental Equipment: Yes.
Instruction: PSIA-certified.
Food Facilities: Snack bar at touring center.
Lodging: At nearby inns and condominiums.
How to Get There: I–91 north of Exit 23; Route 5 to Route 114
   to East Burke; signs to Burke Mountain.

This historic center for Alpine athletes (Burke Ski Academy) also maintains a well-developed touring center over the rolling meadows and deep Vermont woodlands near the Northeast Wilderness Kingdom. Most of the trail system is intermediate, though those same trails have been used for National Cross-Country Championships. From some high-country vantage points, skiers look out for miles to the west and can view the striking scenery of Willoughby Gap, gateway to the Northeast Kingdom. Skiers may use any trail system here and wind back to the center. The Touring Center itself is a friendly, bustling stop in an old restored farmhouse with a radiant wood stove at its center. Here skiers may sip hot cider and homemade soups, rent equipment, buy retail goods, and seek instruction. Children are welcome both at the touring center and at the Cutter Inn, in the midst of the trail network.

BLUEBERRY HILL
RD 3
Goshen, Vermont 05733
(802) 247–6735 or 800–274–6535;
outside Vermont: (800) 448–0707

Hours: 8:30 A.M. to dusk.
Trail System: 50 to 75 kilometers (about 30 to 47 miles), depending on snow cover and forestry activity in the National Forest.
Trail Difficulty: Easiest, more difficult, most difficult.
Trail Grooming: All trails groomed and double trackset. Some skating lanes.
Rental Equipment: Yes.
Instruction: Private and group rates.
Food Facilities: Soup included in the trail fee, along with "munchies," but bring your own packed lunches and other meals.
Lodging: Blueberry Hill is connected with a small inn.
How to Get There: I–91 to I–89 west to Route 4, west to Rutland, Vermont; north on Route 7 to Brandon, east on Route 73 to Goshen, then left at the town hall to Blueberry Hill.

Blueberry Hill, nestled in the Green Mountain National Forest with an honest 50- to 75-kilometer trail system, is a major ski area for the serious tourer as well as the hiker searching for gorgeous mountain overlooks that plunge into deep forest land with snow-laden fir boughs and frozen brooks. Silver Lake trail is a good way to get your legs; then stretch out along Long Trail for more challenging skiing. There is an excellent retail and rental shop at Blueberry, along with waxing rooms where some helpful lessons are given. The inn is small—just eight rooms—but the space is worth fighting for.

Ask for ski director Steve Buskey or owner Tony Clark for special advice about skiing conditions.

GRAFTON PONDS CROSS-COUNTRY SKI CENTER
The Old Tavern at Grafton
Grafton, Vermont 05146
(802) 843–2231

Hours: 9 A.M. to 4 P.M.
Trail System: About 17 kilometers (10 miles).
Trail Difficulty: Easiest, more difficult, most difficult.
Trail Grooming: All trails groomed and trackset, with skating lanes provided.
Rental Equipment: Full rental facility.
Instruction: Private lessons by appointment.
Food Facilities: Formal dining at The Old Tavern with trail snacks available at the center.
Lodging: The Old Tavern has several guest rooms; there are also several motels in the area.
How to Get There: From I–91 take Exit 5 and head west on Route 121. Grafton Ponds is located at the intersection of Route 121 and Route 35.

This area is one of several in Vermont that combines a rich outback experience with modern grooming techniques on the trail and a rustic country inn with gourmet dining after the skiing ends. The trail system has something for everyone, starting with the beginners' and warm-up loops like Strider and Windham Pond Trail: level skiing on broad swaths for confidence-building and loosening. For the intermediate there is the 3-mile New Lee Wilson Trail that meanders through forested hillsides and the 2-mile Warren Chivers Trail that combines a short uphill with a gentler, undulating downhill. The Dinkum-Dankum Area has lots of moderate terrain with the infamous Gorge thrown in to give a sobering snap of reality to anyone nodding off or feeling smug. This latter area has all sorts of surprises and payoffs—like Mathey Lane, an extremely pleasing .7-mile run that brings skiers home after taking the dreaded plunge.

The Old Tavern is a graceful old stagecoach inn dating back to 1801. Restored antique guest rooms and elegant inn dining make this one of Vermont's best bets for destination skiers.

HIGHLAND LODGE
Caspian Lake
Greensboro, Vermont 05841
(802) 533–2647

Hours: 9 A.M. to 5 P.M.
Trail System: About 48 kilometers (30 miles).
Trail Difficulty: Easiest, more difficult.
Trail Grooming: All 30 miles are roller-packed, 5 feet in width;
    10 miles are double trackset.   /
Rental Equipment: Yes.
Instruction: PSIA-certified.
Food Facilities: Full meals plus trail snacks in the ski shop.
Lodging: Eleven rooms at the lodge and two cottages.
How to Get There: I–91 to St. Johnsbury; at Exit 15, Route 2
    west 10 miles to West Danville; northwest on Route 15 to
    Route 16; north on Route 16 to East Hardwick, then west
    to Greensboro.

There are three loops to Highland Lodge's trail system, two of 5
miles and another of 15 miles. All of these course through the
gently rolling pasturelands and evergreen woods that lead down
and sweep the shore of Caspian Lake. The system covers about
25 square miles. Both loops offer some wonderful overlooks of
this lake region and end with a downhill stretch toward a drink
at the fireplace. The trails are conscientiously roller-packed so
skiers don't have to bushwhack their way through deep powder
or crust.

The lodge is a spectacular stately Vermont inn with a broad
homey dining room, library and lounge areas, and good-size
double bedrooms. There is room for thirty-five guests. The inn
hosts loyal families that have been returning for several years.
There is also a thorough ski and rental shop at the center where
skiers may sign up for instruction and guided tours of the region.

CAMEL'S HUMP NORDIC SKI CENTER
Box 422, RFD 1
Huntington, Vermont 05462
(802) 434–2704

Hours: 9 A.M. to 5 P.M.
Trail System: 60 kilometers (about 37 miles).
Trail Difficulty: Easiest, more difficult, most difficult.
Trail Grooming: As needed; 30 kilometers of skating lanes.
Rental Equipment: Yes.
Instruction: Yes.
Food Facilities: Snacks served at the center.
Lodging: Bed-and-breakfast on premises; other lodging nearby.
How to Get There: I–91 to I–89 northwest to Exit 11; 7 miles
   south to Huntington; 3 miles east from Huntington village
   to the touring center.

Of all Vermont's high Alpine ski touring, this Nordic Ski Center just may provide the most dramatic and unusual experience. Though the center itself is a modest, family-run operation, it is located at road's end high in the eastern foothills of the 4,000-foot Camel's Hump and accesses many miles of wilderness as well as providing its own well-groomed trail system of about 37 miles. Here is skiing for everyone: the high energy seeker of wilderness adventure can find guided overnight trips to a snow cave. One trail, the Honey Hollow Ski Trail, climbs to 1,900 feet, then drops 1,500 feet over the west slope on a nonstop downhill run of 9 kilometers to the bank of the Winooski River in Bolton. Skiers needn't climb back up this 5-mile rush through the state forest; the center provides shuttle service back home again. The center intends to complete soon a network of trail huts for overnight skiers who can travel south to Breadloaf and Blueberry Hill.

   For gentler spirits not looking for quite this level of stimulation, the center has plenty of cruising on flatter trails through woods and open mountain uplands. All rentals and retail needs, along with meals, are taken care of in the rustic center, which now also provides lodging.

HEERMANSMITH FARM
RFD 1
Irasburg (Coventry Village), Vermont 05845
(802) 754–8866

Hours: 9 A.M. to 4 P.M.
Trail System: 15 kilometers (about 9½ miles) with three connected trails.
Trail Difficulty: Easiest, more difficult, most difficult.
Trail Grooming: Groomed and trackset daily. Skating lanes on meadow.
Rental Equipment: Yes.
Instruction: No.
Food Facilities: Dinners open to public nightly except Tuesday; lunch and breakfast served to guests only.
Lodging: Six rooms available at the farm.
How to Get There: I–91 to Orleans exit, then north along Route 5 for 5 miles to Coventry Village; the inn is ¼ mile beyond the village.

Heermansmith Farm is 15 miles from the Jay Peak ski area in the remote wilds of northern Vermont. Like the other medium-sized Nordic areas in this region, the farm offers a real variety of groomed tracks and bushwhacking terrain. Former U.S. Ski Team member Stan Dunklee designed the trackset course with its three interconnected trail loops. Starting with the meadow trail cut along flats for a 2-kilometer run, skiers can take off along the Black River trail, which winds along the lovely trout stream, in and out of sun-dappled fir forest. For more serious runners there is the 6-kilometer trail that takes you 2 kilometers uphill, then 4 kilometers down a gentle winding slope through maple orchards. On Sunday evenings, 2 kilometers of trail near the Farm are lighted with luminaries.

JAY PEAK SKI AREA
Route 242
Jay, Vermont 05859
(802) 988–2611 (Customer Service)

Hours: 8:30 A.M. to dusk.
Trail System: About 20 kilometers (13 miles).
Trail Difficulty: Easiest, more difficult, most difficult.
Trail Grooming: As needed.
Rental Equipment: 50 sets.
Instruction: PSIA-certified.
Food Facilities: Cafeteria and two restaurants.
Lodging: Hotel Jay. Call Jay Peak Lodging Association at 800–451–4449, or (802) 988–2611.
How to Get There: I–91 to Exit 26 in Orleans, Vermont; northwest via Routes 5 to 14 to 100, to 101, and to 242 and the entrance.

With its multinational flag row, its mix of languages and cultures, and its large Alpine facility, Jay Peak in the northernmost tip of the state in the Wilderness Kingdom is a most exciting place to spend a ski weekend or vacation. The extensive cross-country trail system incorporates the lower half of Jay Mountain itself, which brings into play some long, gradually pitched Alpine runouts from mid-mountain down to the base. Obviously, Jay is a fine place to work on Telemark skiing, for then skiers can make use of the entire area—including two T-bars (included in trail fee) when none of your cross-country purist pals are watching. The base lodge and restaurant at the Hotel Jay is ample and well stocked. As a diversion from skiing, take the aerial tram to the top of one of the most overwhelming mountain vistas anywhere, as you view the sun dropping toward the Laurentians and Montreal. Don't worry—if you're not up to skiing down the mountain on skinny skis, you may take the tram back down.

RED FOX SKI TOURING CENTER
Old Route 108, Box 26
Jeffersonville, Vermont 05464
(802) 644–8888

Hours: 8 A.M. to 4 P.M.
Trail System: 3 kilometers (about 2 miles) from Red Fox to Smugglers Notch Ski Touring Area; 2 kilometers (about 1¼ miles) along the Brewster River; 17 kilometers (about 10 miles) from Smugglers Notch to Pleasant Valley. A brief bus ride accesses all the trails of Stowe.
Trail Difficulty: Easiest, more difficult.
Trail Grooming: None.
Rental Equipment: No.
Instruction: Yes.
Food Facilities: Breakfast and dinner at the Red Fox Lodge.
Lodging: At the lodge. Capacity of 100; 2, 4, or 6 to a room.
How to Get There: I–89 from Burlington, Vermont, to Exit 15 east; Route 108 south for 4 miles to Red Fox on the left.

Along the Old Mountain road on the way to Smugglers Notch in the northern expanse of the state, a converted church has long served as one of the original ski dormitories in the awesome landscape of Smugglers Notch. This is historic ski country, where the 10th Mountain Army Division trained and where early ski pioneers still live today.

81

The Red Fox Alpine Lodge itself accesses several trail systems and specializes in group accommodations for up to 100 skiers in nice clean rooms of six beds each. The Red Fox places heavy emphasis on teaching the sport both over trails and in the surrounding wilderness settings. This is an excellent region for backcountry bushwhacking and even some extensive—carefully planned—wilderness treks. All of Smugglers' and Stowe's trail systems are at your disposal, and if you happen to commit Alpine skiing, you're in one of the capitals of the Northeast.

STERLING RIDGE INN
RR 1, Box 578C
Jeffersonville, Vermont 05464
(802) 644–8265

Hours: 8 A.M. to 5 P.M.
Trail System: 12 kilometers (about 7 miles).
Trail Difficulty: Easiest, more difficult, most difficult.
Trail Grooming: Groomed and trackset.
Rental Equipment: No.
Instruction: No.
Food Facilities: Breakfast and lunch (or trail packed lunch) daily from the inn; gourmet dinner prepared Saturday, Monday, and Wednesday evenings through ski season.
Lodging: Eight rooms at the inn; shared or private bath available.
How to Get There: Route I–89 to Burlington, then Route 15 to Jeffersonville. From Jeffersonville, 1.2 miles east on Route 15, then right on the dirt road for 1.1 miles; then south on Route 108; turn left by the Red Fox onto an unpaved road for 2.1 miles.

The Sterling Ridge Inn is one of the many fine four-season Vermont inns that maintain a well-groomed cross-country trail system for winter guests. It is located near the renowned cross-country skiing activity of the Stowe area, so skiers staying at Sterling Ridge have many other skiing options in addition to the inn's own 12-kilometer trail system. The skiing at the inn ranges from flattish open-meadow trails that let novices get their bearings to a few more challenging trail loops, one of which leads out to a cabin in the woods along an intermediate trail. Skiers out for the day can take packed lunches from the gourmet kitchen at the inn and return after the most vigorous day of skiing without fear of a calorie deficit. Three nights a week the inn offers its own dinner; otherwise there are several restaurants in the area. Downhill skiing is also available nearby.

MOUNTAIN MEADOWS SKI TOURING CENTER
Box 2080
Killington, Vermont 05751
(802) 775-7077

Hours: 8 A.M. to 6 P.M.
Trail System: 40 kilometers (25 miles).
Trail Difficulty: Easiest, more difficult, most difficult.
Trail Grooming: Daily grooming on all 40 kilometers; 15 kilometers of skating lanes.
Rental Equipment: Yes.
Instruction: PSIA-certified.
Food Facilities: Lunches and snacks at the center.
Lodging: Dormitory and private rooms at the center.
How to Get There: I–93 to I–89 to Exit 2, then west on Route 4 to Killington; right on Thundering Brook Road to Mountain Meadows.

Nestled in a high mountain valley 5 miles away from the famous Killington downhill area, the Mountain Meadows Lodge is a large century-old converted farmhouse and barn that now can accommodate seventy tourers. The trail network, combining the depths of the Green Mountain National Forest with open mountain highlands and the flats of Kent's Pond, has offerings for every ability level. The adventurous can pick up the route along the 40-mile Catamount Ski Touring Trail and follow it into Chittenden to the Mountain Top Ski Touring Center. The shop at Mountain Meadows is fully equipped with

rentals and retail gear, a waxing room, and good advice. Skiers
can sign up here for day or moonlight tours. Beginners should
ask about the Five-Day Learn-to-Ski Week. Two kilometers
near the lodge are lighted for some night running.

NORDIC INN SKI TOURING CENTER
Route 11
Landgrove, Vermont 05148
(802) 824–6444

Hours: 9 A.M. to 4 P.M.
Trail System: About 26 kilometers (15-plus miles).
Trail Difficulty: Easiest, more difficult, most difficult.
Trail Grooming: Trackset daily.
Rental Equipment: 50 sets.
Instruction: Yes.
Food Facilities: Gourmet restaurant (seats 75) and pub at the inn.
Lodging: 5 rooms at the inn; other motels nearby.
How to Get There: I–91 to Exit 6; Route 103 northwest; then
    Route 11 west to Landgrove and the inn.

With its continental French cuisine and pub life, Nordic Inn is
becoming as well known for its après-ski life as for its excellent
trail system. The latter, a thoroughly groomed and trackset web
of trails at over 1,369 feet, leads skiers into the Green National
Forest, where plenty of wilderness skiing is at hand. The inn offers a full service of guided tours, instruction, and various events
through the season. After a day on these broad, hardwood-lined
trails, skiers stretch in front of the huge fieldstone fireplace
that crackles and roars through the long winter evening. This is
a fine destination area for those who like some pampering
when they're off the trails. Nordic Inn is just 3 miles from Londonderry and 5 miles from the Bromley downhill ski area.

VIKING SKI TOURING CENTRE
Little Pond Road, RR Box 70
Londonderry, Vermont 05148
(802) 824-3933

Hours: 8:30 A.M. to 4:30 P.M.
Trail System: 40 kilometers (25 miles).
Trail Difficulty: Easiest, more difficult, most difficult.
Trail Grooming: Yes, trackset.
Rental Equipment: 80 sets.
Instruction: PSIA-certified.
Food Facilities: Meals at the cafe; hot snacks and drinks at the ski center.
Lodging: Inns and hotels in the area.
How to Get There: I-91 to Brattleboro, Vermont; Route 30 northwest, then Route 100 north to Londonderry.

Viking is one of the original New England touring centers, dating back to 1970. It has a variety of offerings for skiers of all levels and like most well-established centers, really emphasizes the proper education of a skier. The trail system is absolutely superb, with intelligently cut and marked trails for every level, and with guided tours out to beautiful remote backlands near Grout Pond in the Green Mountains' Lye Brook Wilderness Area.

Just as it should, the center fixes on skier needs: A complete rental and retail facility is available, along with a waxing room and a warming shack and plenty of advice and discussion about the potion of the day. Lodging and expanded dining facilities are available at any number of inns and hotels in the Manchester/Londonderry area.

RABBIT HILL INN
Lower Waterford, Vermont 05848
(802) 748-5168

Hours: Dawn to dusk.
Trail System: 25 kilometers (about 16 miles).
Trail Difficulty: Easiest, more difficult.

Trail Grooming: Yes.
Rental Equipment: Yes.
Instruction: Limited (call ahead).
Food Facilities: Breakfast and dinner.
Lodging: Twenty rooms with private baths; some with working
    fireplaces.
How to Get There: Route 18 from Littleton, New Hampshire,
    to St. Johnsbury, Vermont; then 6 miles from the termina-
    tion of I–93.
Rabbit Hill's trails meander along the Connecticut River,
through groves of beechwoods, past beaver lodges, and up Rabbit Hill for a look back over the picturesque village anchored by
a white New England meeting house. This is quiet, high-quality skiing away from the masses. Trails cross much private
land, looping through wide meadows that plunge into forested
river bank. The 1795 inn with its twenty bedrooms once served
one hundred horse teams daily that hauled produce from Portland, Maine, to interior New England and Montreal. Nearly all
the rooms have mountain views, and the cuisine, enhanced by
offerings from the inn's own wine cellar, is exquisite. Aside
from skiing, the inn provides guided nature walks and climbs
in the White Mountains.

FOX RUN RESORT
RFD 1, Box 123
Ludlow, Vermont 05149
(802) 228–8871

Hours: 8 A.M. to 5 P.M.
Trail System: 15 kilometers (about 10 miles).
Trail Difficulty: Easiest, more difficult, most difficult.
Trail Grooming: Yes. Some lanes for skating.
Rental Equipment: Yes.
Instruction: Yes.
Food Facilities: Lunch and dinner.
Lodging: At the Winchester Inn, owned by Fox Run, and the
    Okemo Inn across the street; other areas have bed-and-
    breakfast lodging.

How to Get There: Route I–91 to Exit 6, then Route 103 north to Ludlow. One mile north of Okemo access road.

The Fox Run Resort has grown in trail size over the years, so that it now qualifies as a moderately large area with a full-range system through fir-forested terrain that gives skiers some nice views of Okemo Mountain. The trails vary from flat racers to choppy bushwhacking and serious verticals for the expert skier. There is also now a full rental and retail shop available on the premises, as well as instructors who will help you bone up on racing technique or take you on a guided tour of the network. In the inn, the wood beams glowing with the light from copper lamps make a nice ambiance in which to loosen down from the day's skiing.

BIRCH HILL INN
West Road, Box 346
Manchester, Vermont 05254
(802) 362–2761

Hours: Dawn to dusk, as conditions prevail. For inn guests only.
Trail System: 13 kilometers (about 8 miles).
Trail Difficulty: Easiest, more difficult, most difficult.
Trail Grooming: None, except for snowmobile tracks.
Rental Equipment: None.
Instruction: None.
Food Facilities: Only for guests of the inn.
Lodging: At the inn.
How to Get There: Route 30 in the center of Manchester north toward Dorset; left onto Manchester West Road, about ¾ mile to Birch Hill Inn.

This area's 8 miles of gladed trails are maintained exclusively for guests of Birch Hill Inn, one of the most postcard-lovely inns in New England. The skiing begins at a small brook-fed pond that gurgles in and out of woods. The trails—of varying degrees of difficulty—are picturesque, solitary courses through the quiet Vermont woods. On returning, skiers experience the best in New England inn life as proprietor Jim Lee takes you on a tour of the art hangings—many watercolors of skiers. Dinner is a large country affair, as are the breakfasts. Downhill skiing is available nearby at Stratton, Bromley, and Magic, and there are several Nordic centers nearby as well.

HILDENE SKI TOURING CENTER
Box 377
Manchester, Vermont 05254
(802) 362-1788

Hours: 9 A.M. to 4 P.M.
Trail System: 15 kilometers (about 10 miles).
Trail Difficulty: Easiest, more difficult, most difficult.
Trail Grooming: All groomed, 10 kilometers trackset; some skating lanes.
Rental Equipment: Yes.
Instruction: Private and group by arrangement.
Food Facilities: Hot soups and cocoa all week.
Lodging: Motels and inns nearby.
How to Get There: Route 30 north to Manchester Center, Vermont; left onto Route 7A south. Touring center is ½ mile on left, beyond Equinox Hotel.

This historic estate was built by Robert Todd Lincoln, son of President Abraham Lincoln. It is a 412-acre estate with trails meandering about a central warming hut in the old Carriage Barn. One trail features long downhill runs on a gradual slope, and the fields are open for skating. There is something here for the veteran skier as well as the novice, and all phases in between. Special events beyond the skiing include tours of the main house at Christmastime, December 27 to 29.

CARROL AND JANE RIKERT SKI TOURING CENTER
Service Building
Middlebury College
Middlebury, Vermont 05073

Hours: 9 A.M. to 4 P.M.
Trail System: 50 kilometers (about 30 miles).
Trail Difficulty: Easiest, more difficult, most difficult.
Trail Grooming: Groomed and trackset. Skating lanes.
Rental Equipment: Yes.
Instruction: Yes.
Food Facilities: Light snacks and hot drinks at the center; restaurants within 5 miles.
Lodging: Hotels and motels in the area, within 13 miles of the touring center.
How to Get There: I-93 to I-89 to Route 100 in Bethel, Vermont; Route 125 east in Hancock.

The annual Middlebury Winter Carnival Nordic events are staged at this highly manicured touring center—an indication of the quality of the trail system and the grooming, marking, and care of the trails. Set in the Breadloaf Campus at Middlebury, the trails course around the Robert Frost Memorial here in the base of the Green Mountains. Some trails run out to the Snow Bowl, and one direction links up with the Blueberry Hill Touring Center trail system. This area is largely for intermediate skiing with some gentle flats available, too. There are waxes available along with rental and retail gear at the center. A warming hut is on the premises; they serve superb soups.

ALPINE HAVEN
Montgomery Center, Vermont 05471
(802) 326-4567

Hours: 9 A.M. to 4 P.M.
Trail System: 24 kilometers (15 miles).
Trail Difficulty: Easiest, more difficult, most difficult.
Trail Grooming: Groomed by snowmobile.

Rental Equipment: No, but nearby.
Instruction: No, but nearby.
Food Facilities: Restaurant nearby.
Lodging: At the Alpine Meadows Hotel, the Hotel Jay, or among the several chalets in the area.
How to Get There: I–91 to Orleans, Vermont, exit; then Route 105 to Route 101 to the Alpine Haven Condos between Jay Center and Montgomery Center.

To the southwest of Jay Peak, bordering on the immense Northeast Wilderness Kingdom, Alpine Haven offers a landscape of cruising over gentle rollers to the more hilly ruggedness along the side of Jay Peak's alpine terrain. This is secluded skiing in the true northern wilderness, though Telemarkers who wish to practice have the aerial tram at Jay Peak and some long, smooth runouts down the green-circle Alpine trails.

Nearby, the Hotel Jay has fine accommodations for the destination skier, too. This is a region peopled with many Montrealers, and the whole area has a pleasant international feel.

HAZEN'S NOTCH SKI TOURING CENTER
Route 58
Montgomery Center, Vermont 05471
(802) 326-4708

Hours: 9 A.M. to 4:30 P.M.
Trail System: 20 kilometers (about 12 miles) of groomed trails with 75 kilometers of backcountry trails.
Trail Difficulty: Easiest, more difficult, most difficult.
Trail Grooming: Groomed and trackset as needed. Limited skating.
Rental Equipment: Yes.
Instruction: Much individual attention for novice skiers; special introductory clinics for Telemark skiing.
Food Facilities: At the ski chalet.
Lodging: Overnight accommodations at the guest house at the ski center; inns and motels within 1½ miles.
How to Get There: Route I-91 to White River Junction, Vermont; I-89 to Waterbury, Vermont; Route 100 north to Eden, then Route 118 to Montgomery Center; east on Route 58 to Hazen's.

Nestled high in the wild country and heavy snow belt of the Northeast Kingdom, nearly 50 kilometers of trails wind through a mosaic of deep fir forest and mountain meadowland. These fields provide spectacular views of several mountain ranges, while the backcountry trails lead to little villages and into the dramatic Hazen's Notch. Skiers can find lodging at the center where a guest house offers warm, friendly surroundings that seem a haven after skiing in these winter wilds. After a drink and hot homemade food, high-energy skiers can go back out on guided moonlight tours. Lamps are provided. Telemark clinics and slopes for practice are also available. The Touring Center has a wonderful French/English mix that gives this Green Mountain jewel the kind of international feeling that Alpine skiers find at Jay Peak.

VERMONT VOYAGER EXPEDITIONS
Route 242, Box 1010
Montgomery Center, Vermont 05471
(802) 326-4789

"VVE," as its students call it, is not a touring area as such but rather a year-round mountaineering school associated with Jay Peak in the Northeast Wilderness Kingdom in the northern part of the state. It also is part of an elaborate inn-to-inn touring system that is part of the Northern Frontier Ski Region of Vermont.

VVE, founded in 1980, is dedicated to "the conservation of wilderness through the education of its users." VVE provides instruction in the practical end of wilderness skiing, giving individuals or groups the confidence to explore this exciting corner of the sport of cross-country. Before skiers can try the wilderness experience, they must learn it, which means it must be taught. That is what VVE is all about. Skiers can use VVE for their destination, then, under the tutelege of expert outdoorsmen and guides, undertake as much or as little as they feel up to in this vast unspoiled terrain among the northernmost peaks of the Green Mountains, as well as the lowland trails that lead through meadows and farms and in and out of remote northern villages.

THE MONTPELIER ELKS SKI TOURING CENTER
Country Club Road
Montpelier, Vermont 05602
(802) 223-7457

Hours: Weekends, January through March, 9 A.M. to 5 P.M.
Trail System: 8 kilometers (5 miles).
Trail Difficulty: Easiest, more difficult.
Trail Grooming: Packed and trackset as needed.
Rental Equipment: Yes.
Instruction: By appointment.
Food Facilities: Lunch at the Montpelier Elks Club.
Lodging: Several hotels and motels nearby.

How to Get There: I–93 to I–89 to Exit 7, Route 302 to Route 2 east to country club on left. Touring Center is at the top of the hill.

This small, family-oriented touring center in the Barre/Montpelier region is most suited to day touring or as an alternative for Alpine skiers staying in the area. The trails are gently rolling, open-field loops that won't test the expert yet can provide plenty of exercise along the golf-course terrain. Expansion plans are underway at Montpelier Elks that will double the ski acreage. Skiers can use the woods nearby, too.

PROSPECT MOUNTAIN SKI TOURING CENTER
HCR 65 - Box 760
Woodford, Vermont 05201
(802) 442–2575

Hours: 9 A.M. to 5 P.M.
Trail System: 40 kilometers (25 miles).
Trail Difficulty: Easiest, more difficult, most difficult.
Trail Grooming: All tracks are groomed and skateable.
Rental Equipment: 85 sets.
Instruction: Yes.
Food Facilities: Lunch only served at the base lodge.
Lodging: Greenwood Lodge nearby accommodates groups; motels in the area.
How to Get There: Eight miles east of Bennington; 12 miles west of Wilmington on Route 9.

A high-altitude ski touring center (2,150 feet) in the Green Mountains of western Vermont, Prospect Mountain usually retains a snow cover after the flatlands are bare. The area offers as wide a variety as any ski area in New England—from flat running tracks, to wilderness bushwhacking on 20 kilometers of expert terrain on the mountainside. Another 10 kilometers are intermediate; and 10 kilometers are easiest.

Groomed tracks break down to roughly 5 kilometers of most difficult and 10 of more difficult.

WILD WINGS SKI TOURING CENTER
Peru, Vermont 05152
(802) 824–6793

Hours: 9 A.M. to 4 P.M.
Trail System: 20 kilometers (about 13 miles).
Trail Difficulty: Easiest, more difficult, most difficult.
Trail Grooming: Groomed and trackset as needed.
Rental Equipment: Yes.
Instruction: PSIA-certified.
Food Facilities: Hot drinks and snacks in the warming rooms and at nearby restaurants.
Lodging: Tourers can find inns and motels within 3 to 10 miles.
How to Get There: I–91 to Brattleboro, Vermont; Route 30 northwest to Route 11, east to Peru; left at the Peru Church and follow to Wild Wings.

Still in the Green Mountain National Forest, this is a small, extremely cozy sort of area out of some of the touring bustle or the hotshot race crowd in skin-tight suits. In a converted horse barn you'll find a rental shop and warming/waxing room, then go out skiing over 10 to 12 miles of groomed trails. This system feeds into the vast Green Mountain trail system as well. This home of the wild turkey is one of the prettiest ski regions in New England.

WILDERNESS TRAILS AND NORDIC SKI SCHOOL
c/o The Quechee Inn
Quechee, Vermont 05059
(802) 295–7620; Off-season, (802) 295–3133.

Hours: 9 A.M. to dark.
Trail System: 15 kilometers (about 9 miles).
Trail Difficulty: Easiest, more difficult, most difficult.
Trail Grooming: Machine trackset.
Rental Equipment: Yes.
Instruction: Two PSIA-certified instructors.

Food Facilities: A trailside restaurant, Red Pines, serves hot chocolate, coffee, and snacks. Breakfast and dinner are available at the inn.

Lodging: Twenty-two units at the inn; other motels nearby.

How to Get There: I–93 north to I–89; at White River Junction, Exit 1, Route 4 west toward Woodstock, and follow signs to Quechee. At the sign, right onto Clubhouse Road; 1 mile to the inn.

The touring at Quechee is among the most beautiful anywhere, with the most spectacular trail running along the rim of Quechee Gorge. Here, a waterfall plunges 165 feet down into the gorge. Skiers are treated to a wildlife area where sightings of mink, otter, beaver, fox, and porcupines are common. For birders, there are rare pileated woodpeckers in the trees, as well as owls that are sometimes encountered on moonlight tours. Ask for Marty Banak for tips on the wildlife tour. Generally, Wilderness Trails is a nice low-key sort of area known mostly for its emphasis on teaching. In the Woodstock area, there is plenty of skiing (both Nordic and Alpine); the whole region offers nightlife and shopping.

GREEN MOUNTAIN TOURING CENTER
At the Three Stallion Inn
Randolph, Vermont 05060
(802) 728–5575

Hours: Dawn to dusk.

Trail System: 35 kilometers (about 21 miles).

Trail Difficulty: Easiest, more difficult, most difficult.

Trail Grooming: Daily. Trackset and skating track.

Rental Equipment: Yes.

Instruction: Yes.

Food Facilities: Meals served to guests in the farmhouse.

Lodging: Fifteen rooms at the farmhouse, other inns and motels in the area.

How to Get There: I–93 to I–89 north to Exit 4; then Route 66 west; left on Stock Farm Road to the touring center.

The Green Mountain Touring Center is one of those no-nonsense, homey resorts that call to skiers who seek the simplicity of a fine trail system, good hot homemade food, and plenty of hospitality in a Victorian farmhouse inn. This center seems to weed out the essential pleasures of the sport from the frills that merely cost money and get in the way. Skiers at Green Mountain will find a big, conscientiously groomed and marked trail system spread out on nearly 1,400 acres of Green Mountain forest land where more than a few U.S. Ski Team members have trained over the years. The terrain rolls along gentle ridges and plunges into woods that can offer skiers any level of vertical ups and downs. For novices there are plenty of flat trails as well. At the center are a cocktail lounge and restaurant open to the public at lunch and dinner. Look into this inn as a four-season destination.

NORDIC ADVENTURES
Connie and Dean Mendell
Box 155, RFD 1
Rochester, Vermont 05767
(802) 767-3996

Hours: To be arranged.
Trail System: Any and all accessible lands can be used.
Trail Difficulty: Easiest, more difficult.
Trail Grooming: Foot-packed or groomed with snowmobile.
Rental Equipment: 50 sets of waxable backcountry skis.
Instruction: PSIA-certified instructor.
Food Facilities: A country lunch is offered on guided tours.
Lodging: Inns in the area.
How to Get There: I–93 to I–89 north to the exit at Bethel, Vermont; then Route 107 to Route 100 north. The Mendell's house is 4 miles south of Rochester Village on Route 100 North.

Nordic Adventures is an outfitter and guide system that offers personalized instruction on a one-to-one basis. Skiers interested in backcountry forays have a choice of several package plans, including inn-to-inn ski hikes, Norpine instruction, and moon-light escapades. A typical five-day package in the $500 range would include lodging, all meals, guide and instruction fees, luggage transfer, taxes, and gratuities. This is a different approach to touring than the ordinary destination trip and should appeal to skiers who really like to probe into the woolly corners of the sport. Mr. Mendell knows the woods and can personally arrange a wilderness tour to fit individual skiers' tastes and abilities.

TRAIL HEAD SKI TOURING
Star Route
Stockbridge, Vermont 05772
(802) 746-8038

Hours: 9 A.M. to 5 P.M.
Trail System: 45 kilometers (about 28 miles).
Trail Difficulty: Easiest, more difficult, most difficult.
Trail Grooming: Partially; machine-set on beginner to interme-
   diate terrain; most of the expert trails foot-packed.
Rental Equipment: Yes.
Instruction: Yes.
Food Facilities: Homemade soups, snacks, drinks, and sand-
   wiches in the lodge. Restaurants in the area for dinners.
Lodging: Seven lodging establishments within five minutes of
   the area.
How to Get There: I-93 to I-89 to Route 107 in Vermont; then
   to Route 100 south for 1 mile to the touring center.

Near Rutland, Vermont, the Trail Head Touring Center is a large system in the Green Mountain National Forest offering a variety of touring experiences. Skiers can warm up with open-meadow cruising over well-set tracks, then roll down along the lovely Tweed River trails that course in and out of deep woods. More advanced skiers have the option of some real pumping terrain along the South Hill or out to the Liberty Hill System. Most of the ski terrain offers some nice glimpses of the nearby Alpine terrain. Back at the lodge, a converted barn from the

1870s, cold, tired skiers lounge in front of the roaring fire sipping drinks and homemade soups. Here they find a complete rental and retail facility and can sign up for lessons with PSIA-certified instructors or citizen races. Also available are moonlit excursions through the river valley and over the pastureland. With Killington Ski Area nearby, there is plenty of nightlife for the indefatigable skier, as well as good lodging and dining. Trail Head is an excellent day- or destination trip for skiers of every level.

EDSON HILL MANOR
Edson Hill Road
Stowe, Vermont 05672
(802) 253-7371

Hours: 9 A.M. to 5 P.M.
Trail System: 40 kilometers (25 miles).
Trail Difficulty: Easiest, more difficult, most difficult.
Trail Grooming: Daily, as needed. Skating on 10 percent.
Rental Equipment: Yes.
Instruction: Yes.
Food Facilities: At the Manor house.
Lodging: Rooms of two to three beds at the Manor house.
How to Get There: I–91 and I–89 northwest to Exit 10; Route 100 north to Stowe Village; Route 108 west; take the right fork on Edson Hill Road to the Manor.

This rather overlooked, under-publicized area has a mammoth trail system, few crowded days, and gorgeous terrain for first-out novices and old hands alike. The trails, spread out over a 400-acre estate, are contained in flat, gladed meadowland. Then the fun begins, as skiers climb off the flats, if they wish, into some backland touring in the rugged Green Mountain terrain. The wax shop is complete and has a nice feel of the horse barn that it serves as in the warm season. Here skiers can obtain retail gear of all kinds, rent skis, try to get words of free advice from the experts all around, or put down a little cash for a real lesson. The Edson Hill Manor itself is not quite in the character of the old Vermont inn tour yet is extremely relaxing, gentle, and stress-removing. The food is fine, the atmosphere bright and supple. Also available to skiers is a country inn. Sleigh rides and horseback riding are available year-round.

MT. MANSFIELD SKI TOURING CENTER
Mountain Road
Stowe, Vermont 05672
(802) 253-7311, ext. 2243

Hours: 9 A.M. to 4 P.M.
Trail System: 50 kilometers (about 31 miles).
Trail Difficulty: Easiest, more difficult, most difficult.
Trail Grooming: Grooming on 30 kilometers; unlimited wilderness access; skating.
Rental Equipment: Yes.
Instruction: Yes.
Food Facilities: Full-service restaurant at the base lodge, and several restaurants on the road between Mansfield and Stowe. Snacks at the touring center.
Lodging: At the Inn at the Mountain.
How to Get There: Route I-89 to Exit 10; then 10 miles north on Route 100 to Stowe Village; left on Route 108 for 5 miles.

Always noted as one of the ski capitals of the East, Stowe's 50 kilometers of mapped Nordic trails (30 kilometers are groomed and trackset) live up to that reputation. Mt. Mansfield offers a variety of terrain for every ability level in acreage that plunges deep into the solitude and beauty of the Green Mountains. Because it intersects with other trail systems, skiers from Mt. Mansfield actually have 150 kilometers of trails at their disposal.

Using both sides of the historic Ranch Valley up the flanks of Mt. Mansfield, these trails are exceptionally well maintained, forming a complex that provides the basis for the famous Stowe Derby—an annual 12-mile trot from the top of Mansfield into the village of Stowe. Wilderness trails connect with the Trapp Family Lodge complex, allowing a full day of touring or wilderness exploration.

TOPNOTCH TOURING CENTER
Mountain Road
Stowe, Vermont 05672
(802) 253–8585

Hours: 9 A.M. to 5 P.M.
Trail System: 30 kilometers (about 20 miles).
Trail Difficulty: Easiest, more difficult, most difficult.
Trail Grooming: 20 kilometers groomed daily; skating.
Rental Equipment: Yes.
Instruction: Yes.
Food Facilities: The entire Stowe area is a culinary delight.
Lodging: Dozens of inns and motels in the town of Stowe.
How to Get There: I–89 to Route 100 north; then Route 108 northwest. Topnotch is between Stowe Village and Mountain Mansfield, 4 miles from the village.

Like all ski centers of this region, the town of Stowe itself is the draw here for the destination skier. Our advice is to book trips well ahead, especially in busy seasons. The inn itself features lodging toward the luxury end of the spectrum and dining to match in this very competitive restaurant area. The trail system, though it does offer some trails in the "most difficult" category, is geared toward less stressful skiing. The Lower and Upper Valley Trails send skiers over some rugged terrain that eventually makes a link with Trapp Lodge's trail system. Another route along some much easier terrain ties skiers in with the Edson Hill Manor trails. Yet another route (Cross Cut) winds skiers into the Mt. Mansfield downhill area for some Telemark practice. For the less adventurous, the trails close to the Topnotch Center itself are nicely groomed, gentle rollers that run along open meadows, through woodland, and along the West Branch River. Topnotch is an excellent spot for both the casual and the more serious skier. For beginners there is an abundance of open-field, flat skiing.

TRAPP FAMILY LODGE
Stowe, Vermont 05672
(802) 253–8511

Hours: 9 A.M. to 5 P.M.
Trail System: About 96 kilometers (60 miles).
Trail Difficulty: Easiest, more difficult, most difficult.
Trail Grooming: Groomed and trackset on 60 kilometers; skating lanes.
Rental Equipment: 400 sets.
Instruction: PSIA-certied.
Food Facilities: Restaurant and lounge; lunches served at cabin or on the trail system.
Lodging: Ninety-three rooms on premises.
How to Get There: I–91 (or I–93) to I–89, northwest to Exit 10; Route 100 north to Stowe.

The famous Trapp Family Lodge is still credited as the origin of Nordic skiing in America. Its fabled setting—and historical background—make it the best-known touring capital in the East and perhaps the best commercial touring operation in the country.

The well-groomed and -marked trail system stretches out over 1,700 acres of Green Mountain terrain and offers diversity that ranges from open golf-course terrain to wooded thickets to real wilderness skiing, where it borders on the limitless. Obviously, there is a wide variety of skill levels offered here, and the Trapps provide excellent private or group skiing lessons. The site of many collegiate and world-class races, the lodge also offers racing seminars and back-country tours.

While there is lodging at the Trapp Family Lodge, it is usually booked months in advance, but there is plenty of lodging throughout Stowe village, along with some extremely precious nightlife. There are weekly races for lodge guests.

STRATTON MOUNTAIN CROSS-COUNTRY CENTER
Stratton Mountain, Vermont 05155
(802) 297–1880 or (802) 297–2200, Extension 2445.

Hours: 8:30 A.M. to 4 P.M.
Trail System: 32 kilometers (20 miles).
Trail Difficulty: Easiest, most difficult.
Trail Grooming: Daily, in two areas; skating.
Rental Equipment: 160 sets.
Instruction: Yes.
Food Facilities: Tenderloins Restaurant serves lunch and dinner; entertainment on weekends.
Lodging: Inns and motels available; call the Stratton reservation service at (802) 222–1300.
How to Get There: I–91 to Brattleboro, Vermont; Route 30 northwest to Bondville, then left onto the Stratton Mountain access road.

Ski touring at Stratton is like most other things at Stratton, including the Alpine skiing, golf, and tennis: in a word, classy. Stratton is a smooth operation where skiers tour on a smooth and rolling golf course and along wooded trails with pretty views of Stratton Mountain itself and Bromley and Magic mountains. The meandering trails roll through the foothills of the Alpine slopes, some groomed with some others left open.

Stratton's center grooms and tracks 20 miles of trails that take skiers through a variety of experiences, from flat-track running to big rolling heart-stoppers. There are some excellent wilderness trails on the National Forest Terrain—all free. All the rest of Stratton is excellent skiing, well marked and leading to a finely appointed lodge for fire, food, drink, and plenty of talk about the wax you should have used. There are good snacks at the center. By reservation there is a guided tour of Stratton Pond, and throughout the winter there is a cross-country ski festival with plenty of factory vendors and ski reps. Full resort and sports facilities are available nearby.

TUCKER HILL SKI TOURING CENTER
Tucker Hill Lodge
RFD 1, Box 147
Waitsfield, Vermont 05673
(802) 496–3983; toll-free (800) 451–4580

Hours: 9 A.M. to 5 P.M.
Trail System: 45 kilometers (about 27 miles), plus backcountry trails.
Trail Difficulty: Easiest, more difficult, most difficult.
Trail Grooming: Yes, regularly. Some untracked.
Rental Equipment: Skis, including Telemark; snowshoes.
Instruction: PSIA-certified.
Food Facilities: Breakfast, lunch, and dinner at Tucker Hill Lodge. Snacks at the touring center.
Lodging: Twenty rooms at the Tucker Hill Lodge; also available at Plum Creek.
How to Get There: I–93 to I–89 to Route 100 south to Waitsfield; then Route 17 west to Tucker Hill Lodge, about 2 miles.

The Tucker Hill Center is connected to the Sugarbush/Rossignol Ski Touring Center and also the Mad River Nordic Center. The cooperative effort of these areas does much to promote ski touring at a high level; a five-day pass can be obtained to cover the four centers. This southern Vermont area has an extensive, varied, and well-groomed trail network with an emphasis on wooded terrain geared mostly toward the intermediate skier. There's not much here to curl the toes, nor is there much flat-track open terrain for beginners. The trails run over ancient logging roads, and one route leads to the woods-bound Plum Creek, where skiers can find a hot meal and spend the night.

OLE'S CROSS COUNTRY
Airport Road
Warren, Vermont 08674
(802) 496–3430

Hours: 9 A.M. to 5 P.M.
Trail System: 40 kilometers (25 miles).
Trail Difficulty: Easiest, more difficult, most difficult.
Trail Grooming: More than 20 kilometers.
Rental Equipment: Yes.
Instruction: Group and private.
Food Facilities: Cafeteria has hot soups and sandwiches.
Lodging: Nearby.
How to Get There: I–89 north to Exit 3; Route 107 south to
    Route 100, then north to Warren; right on Brook Road, then
    left onto Roxbury Gap Road, then left again into Ole's.

When the Warren-Sugarbush Airport closes for the winter, that's when Ole Mosesen, a fishing guide from Norway, begins setting tracks throughout the airport terrain—fields and gentle-to-tough woodlands—and gets out the waxes to teach novices what they're about. After his waxing clinics—occasionally involving U.S. Ski Team members—Ole serves a hot lunch to skiers at his cafe. The trail system here is a scenic network through the Mad River Valley with six interconnecting trail loops that range from a 2-mile exercise loop to some heavily pitched verticals for the tough runners. One trail, a 16-kilometer bash through the woods, known as Holly King trail, will leave the most seasoned tourer both exhilarated and beat. Beyond this for the real experts is Scrag Mountain. Full retail and rentals are available.

SUGARBUSH INN/ROSSIGNOL SKI TOURING CENTER

Access Road
Warren, Vermont 05674
(802) 583–2301

Hours: 9 A.M. to 5 P.M.
Trail System: 30 kilometers (about 20 miles).
Trail Difficulty: Easiest, more difficult, most difficult.
Trail Grooming: Groomed and double trackset daily; skating lanes.
Rental Equipment: Yes.
Instruction: Yes.
Food Facilities: Across the street from the touring center at the Sugarbush Inn. Full-service restaurant at the golf course, 1½ miles from the center.
Lodging: The inn has forty-six rooms.
How to Get There: I–93 to I–89 north to Exit 9 at Warren/Waitsfield, Vermont; Route 100 to Warren, then left onto the Sugarbush Valley Access Road; the center is 2 miles on the left.

Located in the skirts of the Green Mountains, the Sugarbush/Rossignol center is a complete, expertly operated and maintained cross-country facility that appeals equally to the racing expert and the recreational skiing family. The center offers 20 kilometers of meticulously groomed and marked trails that vary the experience greatly. You can choose the open-field skiing along the flats of the golf course, or the long, fairly gentle wooded run along German Flats Road to the Tucker Hill Touring Center.

At the touring center, you can sign up for lessons at any level. The center can even arrange a demonstration ride on some Rossignol racing skis for those who want to pursue the go-fast end of the sport. The center has a full retail/rental facility and waxing rooms.

TIMBER CREEK SKI TOURING CENTER
Box 860
West Dover, Vermont 05356
(802) 464–0999

Hours: 9:00 A.M. to 4:30 P.M.
Trail System: 14 kilometers (about 9 miles).
Trail Difficulty: Easiest, more difficult, most difficult.
Trail Grooming: Groomed and trackset.
Rental Equipment: Yes.
Instruction: Yes.
Food Facilities: Restaurant within 1 mile. Light snacks and
    drinks at the center.
Lodging: Condominiums at Timber Creek; motels and hotels
    in the area.
How to Get There: I–91 to Route 9 west to Brattleboro; west for
    20 miles to Wilmington, Vermont; Route 100 for 8 miles to
    Mt. Snow entrance; touring center is across the street.

This ski-touring center across from Mt. Snow, with its
panoramic view toward Wilmington Valley, provides for all
skiers' needs and desires. The touring varies from old logging
trails across rolling terrain, to open flats and manicured tracks,
to skiing in the woolly wilderness of these parts. There are
frozen streams and rivers in the woods, deep pine groves, and
stands of hardwood. Timber Creek may be small, but it is expanding in its trail-system size. The center has a full retail and
rental operation with a big waxing room. Skiers who want to
try some Telemark turning, or simply Alpine skiing, can take a
free shuttle across to Mt. Snow.

WINDHAM HILL INN & TOURING CENTER
West Townshend, Vermont 05359
(802) 874–4080

Hours: Dawn to 8 P.M.
Trail System: 8 kilometers (5 miles) of groomed skiing; unlim-
    ited wilderness skiing.

Trail Difficulty: Easiest, more difficult.
Trail Grooming: Yes, packed.
Rental Equipment: Yes; available free for guests.
Instruction: Yes.
Food Facilities: Meal service for guests of the inn.
Lodging: Fifteen guest rooms with private baths.
How to Get There: I–91 to Exit 2 and Brattleboro, Vermont;
   Route 30 north for 22 miles to West Townshend and Wind-
   ham Hill.

This restored nineteenth-century family farmhouse in southern
Vermont is a lovely setting for destination skiers who like pri-
marily wilderness skiing over meadows and through woods.
The inn itself, run by Linda and Ken Busteed, offers full amenities for most skiers' tastes, and more: It is rich in antiques and
Oriental rugs, handmade quilts, and original paintings—the
charms of a past age. The skiing facility is for the exclusive use
of guests. There are no trail fees nor any charge for equipment
use. Aside from its own small groomed network, Windham Hill
has wild open lands, mostly of the gentle-contour variety. This
skiing feeds onto other trail systems like Tater Hill, Viking,
Stratton, and Wild Wings. Trails are for guests only.

CATAMOUNT FAMILY CENTER
421 Governor Chittenden Road
Williston, Vermont 05495
(802) 879–6001

Hours: Sunday, Monday, and Tuesday, 9 A.M. to dusk; Wednes-
   day through Saturday, 9 A.M. to 9 P.M.
Trail System: 40 kilometers (25 miles).
Trail Difficulty: Easiest, more difficult, most difficult.
Trail Grooming: More than 30 kilometers as needed, single
   trackset; skating lanes.
Rental Equipment: 70 sets.
Instruction: PSIA-certified.
Food Facilities: Hot drinks and trail snacks at the center;
   restaurants available within 3 miles.

Lodging: Bed-and-breakfast inns and hotels within 2 miles; Burlington, Vermont, is 8 miles away.
How to Get There: I–93 to I–89 to Vermont Exit 12, then north; right at the second traffic light; 4 miles to the center.

This fifth-generation family farm outside Burlington typifies the kind of old-world solid roots at the center of much of Vermont's charm. The well-groomed and -marked trail system makes gentle loops over fields and woods in the Champlain Valley and offers wonderful sudden views of Camel's Hump and Mt. Mansfield. Though the grade varies just 300 feet vertically throughout the network, there are still a few huff-and-puffers like Ridge Run and Skidway that throw you twisting, quick descents. There are heated trail shelters out on the loop. At night, 3 kilometers are lit for running. The center is in a circa 1796 farmhouse.

HERMITAGE CROSS-COUNTRY TOURING CENTER
Coldbrook Road
Wilmington, Vermont 05363
(802) 464–3511

Hours: 9 A.M. to 4 P.M.
Trail System: 50 kilometers (about 31 miles).
Trail Difficulty: Easiest, more difficult, most difficult. Telemark trails.
Trail Grooming: Most trails, as needed.
Rental Equipment: Yes.
Instruction: Yes.
Food Facilities: Full meals and trail snacks.
Lodging: At the inn (twenty-nine rooms).
How to Get There: I–91 to Brattleboro, Vermont; west on Route 9 to Wilmington.

Two thousand feet up in the Vermont sky, The Hermitage has plenty of snow and touring, generally in woods and stream beds sheltered from the wind. The Ridge Trails run from the top of Haystack Ski Area to the top of Mt. Snow, a 5-mile trek through the National Forest. This is a special springtime challenge for expert skiers and must be guided. In March there are several challenge races at the area as well. There is also good beginner skiing along the flat floor of the Mt. Snow Valley, and intermediates can climb up along the shoulders of the mountains. Like so many Vermont inns, the Hermitage is reconstructed from an eighteenth-century farmhouse and offers the kind of quaint charm tourers look for in such places. The 50 kilometers of marked and groomed trails circle from the inn out to Mt. Snow. The touring center offers full retail and rental services and trail snacks including wine and cheese.

INN AT QUAIL RUN
Smith Road
Wilmington, Vermont 05363
(802) 464–3362

Hours: Daylight.
Trail System: Inn at Quail Run is tied in with the Sitzmark Ski Touring Center with its 35 kilometers (about 21 miles) of trails. Total network is 50 kilometers (about 30 miles).
Trail Difficulty: More difficult.
Trail Grooming: Packed and trackset as needed.
Rental Equipment: Nearby.
Instruction: Nearby.
Food Facilities: Gourmet cuisine for lodge guests; full bar and lodge facility for guests.
Lodging: Contemporary rooms with private baths available.
How to Get There: I–91 from Brattleboro, Vermont; Route 9 west to Wilmington; then Route 100 north for 4 miles to the town center.

This is a small inn straight out of a romantic novel. It sits nearly 2,000 feet up in the southern Green Mountains with some terrific views of this rolling range and of peaks such as Mt. Snow and Haystack. These latter locations are full-blown Alpine areas. Cross-country skiers have 30 miles of private trails at their disposal, all of them starting at the door of the inn. There are plenty of flats for beginners to get their ski legs and the well seasoned to do some warm-up runs before plunging into the special Wilderness trail that runs through snow-coated woodlands, cellar holes filled with rich history, and ponds with beaver lodges and other wildlife—even some beech trees with bear claw marks scratched in the side. If, after the long wilderness tour or the run through the flattish meadows, skiers have anything left in them, the area is near the rollicking Mt. Snow with its celebrated nightlife. This can be embraced or avoided, as skiers wish.

SITZMARK LODGE
Wilmington, Vermont 05363
(802) 464–5498

Hours: 9 A.M. to 5 p.m
Trail System: 35 kilometers (about 22 miles).
Trail Difficulty: Easiest, more difficult, most difficult.

Trail Grooming: Groomed daily, with 6 kilometers of skating lanes.
Rental Equipment: Yes.
Instruction: PSIA-certified.
Food Facilities: Meals served at The Barn Lounge, weekends and holidays.
Lodging: Inns and hotels in the area.
How to Get There: I–91 to Brattleboro, Vermont; Route 9 west to Wilmington; 4 miles north on Route 100 to Sitzmark.

Cross-country skiers at Sitzmark enjoy some spectacular views of the Mt. Snow and Haystack mountain range to the west of the center, as they glide over a wide variety of trails. From the slow rollers, to choppers such as Ponderosa View, this trail system offers something to all levels. Advanced skiers can climb into some stunning mountain plateaus surrounding the center, while novice skiers get their training on an 18-hole golf course and attendant pasture trails.

THE WHITE HOUSE TOURING CENTER
Route 9, P.O. Box 757
Wilmington, Vermont 05363
(802) 464–2136

Hours: 9 A.M. to 4:30 P.M.
Trail System: 45 kilometers (about 27 miles).
Trail Difficulty: Easiest, more difficult, most difficult.
Trail Grooming: Consistently over 30 kilometers.
Rental Equipment: 100 sets.
Instruction: Video lessons available.
Food Facilities: Continental dining at the White House plus skiers' lunches on weekends. Open to the public.
Lodging: Twelve rooms at the White House.
How to Get There: I–91 to Brattleboro, Vermont; Route 9 west to Wilmington and junction of Route 100.

The White House itself, set in the Mt. Snow region, is a turn-of-the-century mansion steeped in Vermont's rural hospitality. With full health spa, sauna, and indoor pool available, and truly exquisite continental cuisine served before roaring fires, this is a place to come home to after a day on the trail. Eight rooms are in the main inn, and four are in the north wing.

The trails are skewed toward intermediates, but there is plenty for the novice and expert as well. Skiing begins with undulating meadow skiing over nicely groomed tracks and progresses to toe-curling downhills over the twisting Raponda Primitive Trail. Not for everyone, this is nevertheless a special run feeding into the Ridge Trail that goes between Haystack and Mt. Snow and offers wonderful vistas of each.

HILLTOP CROSS-COUNTRY CENTER
Box 2820
Wolcott, Vermont 05680
(802) 888–3710

Hours: Saturdays, Sundays, and holidays from 9 A.M. to 5 P.M.
Trail System: 20 kilometers (about 12 miles).
Trail Difficulty: Easiest, more difficult, most difficult.
Trail Grooming: Yes.
Rental Equipment: Yes.
Instruction: No.
Food Facilities: None at the center; restaurant within 3 miles.
Lodging: Within 5 miles.
How to Get There: Route I–92 to I–89 to Route 15.

This small area north of Stowe Village offers good skiing, mostly of the gentle meadow variety, though there is one cranker that sends skiers twisting up and down through the woods. It is very much a locals' area or perhaps a day trip off the beaten path for visitors at Stowe who want to escape the crush. Though the facilities are not for most destination skiers, this is still the luscious land area of northern Vermont, and the trails are an excellent combination of old logging roads and open flats.

WOODSTOCK SKI TOURING CENTER
At the Woodstock Country Club
Route 106
Woodstock, Vermont 05091
(802) 457-2114

Hours: 9 A.M. to dusk.
Trail System: 75 kilometers (about 47 miles).
Trail Difficulty: Least difficult, more difficult, most difficult.
Trail Grooming: 58 kilometers groomed and double-trackset, or
    groomed for skating, daily.
Rental Equipment: Yes.
Instruction: PSIA-certified.
Food Facilities: Restaurant and bar at the center and at the
    Woodstock Inn; indoor sports center 1 mile from center.
Lodging: Inns and motels in the region.
How to Get There: I-91 to I-89; west to Route 4; west to Route
    106; then south to the touring center.

In the heart of this most tweedy Rock Resort (for owner Lau-
rance Rockefeller) town of Woodstock, Vermont—where skiing
all got organized in America some five decades ago under the
agreeable patriarchy of Dartmouth College—this touring area
offers an extensive trail system to skiers who can do without
roughing it or the "wilderness experience." It is rather tuned to
those vacationers seeking the pleasures of ski touring within
the resort experience. Woodstock itself, with the famous inn at
its center, is considered by many one of the loveliest towns in
New England.

That said, it is possible for the serious tourer to take off
from the touring center on a 10-mile trek: Skyline Trail—the
oldest trail in the nation cut specifically for cross-country touring. This deposits skiers in the town of East Barnard. Of the 75
miles of mapped trails, 58 are trackset and groomed daily.
Thirty kilometers are on Mt. Tom, and another 25 wind round
Mt. Peg. There are also golf-course skiing and woods trails.

The Touring Center offers one of the most extensive base
facilities in New England. It is wonderfully large and replete
with a big, steamy shower room, rental shop, ski shop, restaurant, lounge with fireplace, and a large waxing porch. For skiers

in fear of overexpending their energy, there is one trail loop that brings you mercifully close to the back door of the Woodstock Inn. Here, for a mere pittance, you can park your skis and start a hot and huge brunch with salmon bisque against a background of Mozart études.

NEW HAMPSHIRE

New Hampshire

Numbers on map refer to towns numbered below.

1. Bretton Woods, *Bretton Woods Ski Touring Center* 120
2. Chesterfield, *Road's End Farm* 121
3. Conway, *The Darby Field Inn* 122
4. Dixville Notch, *The Balsams Wilderness* 123
5. Dunbarton, *Valley View Country Club* 125
6. Etna, *Moose Mountain Lodge* 126
7. Francestown, *Tory Pines* 127
8. Franconia, *Cannon Mountain* 128
     Franconia Inn Cross-Country Ski Center 129
9. Gorham, *AMC Pinkham Notch Camp* 130
10. Grantham, *Eastman Ski Touring Center* 131
11. Intervale, *Intervale Nordic Ski Touring Center* 132
12. Jackson, *Jackson Ski Touring Foundation* 132
13. Jaffrey, *Shattuck Inn Nordic Ski Center* 134
     Woodbound Inn 135
14. Laconia, *Gunstock Cross-Country Center* 135
15. Lincoln, *Loon Mountain Cross-Country Center* 136
16. New Durham, *Perry Hollow Cross-Country Center* 137
17. New Ipswich, *Windblown Ski Touring* 138
18. New London, *Norsk Cross-Country Ski Center* 138
19. Ossipee, *Deer Cap Ski Touring Center* 139
20. Peterborough, *Temple Mountain Ski Touring* 140
21. Snowville, *Snowvillage Inn* 141
22. Sugar Hill, *Sunset Hill Touring Center* 142
23. Troy, *The Inn at East Hill Farm* 144
24. Waterville Valley, *Waterville Valley Cross-Country Ski Area* 145
25. Wolfeboro, *The Nordic Skier* 146

BRETTON WOODS SKI TOURING CENTER
Bretton Woods, New Hampshire 03575
(603) 278–5181

Hours: 8:30 A.M. to 4:30 P.M.
Trail System: 75 kilometers (about 46 miles).
Trail Difficulty: Least difficult, more difficult, most difficult.
Trail Grooming: Single track with skating lanes on half the trail system.
Rental Equipment: Yes.
Instruction: PSIA-certified.
Food Facilities: Food and drink available at the Touring Center cafeteria, Alpine base lodge, Darby's Tavern, and Fabyan's.
Lodging: At the Bretton Woods Lodge or Rosebrook Townhouses near the Touring Center.
How to Get There: I–93 to Lincoln, New Hampshire; bear right on Route 3 to Twin Mountain, then right on Route 302 at light; the center is 4 miles on the left, across from the Alpine area.

Coursing through the western valley of Mt. Washington, this spectacular, 75-kilometer trail system is truly all things for all skiers, from the raw neophyte seeking a leisurely walk through the White Mountain National Forest, to the serious racer looking to train on tracks graced in the past by such world-class runners as Bill Koch, Tim and Jennifer Caldwell, and Beth Paxson. The U.S. Team held its 1982 Nationals here, and the area hosts an annual stop on the Great American Ski Chase marathon series.

Do no be scared off by all this heaviness, however. Bretton Woods's bread and butter is still the casual touring skier, and the area gears itself to just that. A very well marked trail system offers courses of various lengths and degrees of difficulty, from the broad flats of the golf course on which is located that gorgeous antique, the Mt. Washington Hotel, to the Coronary Hill system, which winds into foothills of the Presidential Range. There are three separate but interlocking trail systems at Bretton Woods—the Ammonoosuc, Deception (for Mount Deception), and Stickney—the latter incorporating the Alpine area and offering the most hilly and tough terrain. You'll do well to stay away from the Cog Railway Road since this is a major snowmobile route.

120

Bretton Woods has lately moved its touring center into a much larger building with full and very well appointed accommodations—a large restaurant and waxing room, a full rental operation, a ski school, and some just-hanging-around space to let skiers thaw the ice out of their beards.

Though skiers can jump on trails from the roadside anywhere around the White Mountain National Forest here, this is not advised for folks unfamiliar with the area. It is vast. The trail system is bewildering. Part of the trail fee pays for the plasticized maps you pick up at the touring center, which offer advice about shelters along the trail and the level of difficulty for the various routes. The area is on the opposite side of Mt. Washington from Jackson, and as the sun sets on a winter afternoon, the mountain holds the light longer in the sky as it blinks through the spectrum—orange to red to violet to blue. If Jackson is the place to watch the winter sunrise, then Bretton Woods is the spot to view amazing sunsets. Overnight and moonlight excursions are available.

The area has a limited number of beds at this point—less than one hundred—including existing Rosebrook townhouses and The Lodge motel, but motels are available down Route 302 toward Twin Mountain.

ROAD'S END FARM
Jackson Hill Road
Chesterfield, New Hampshire 03443
(603) 363-4703

Hours: 9 A.M. to 5 P.M.
Trail System: 32 kilometers (about 19 miles).
Trail Difficulty: Easiest, more difficult, most difficult.
Trail Grooming: Trackset.
Rental Equipment: Yes.
Instruction: Weekends, holidays, and school vacations.
Food Facilities: Sandwiches, soup, and snacks available on
    weekends, holidays, and vacations.
Lodging: Inns and motels in the area, and at the farm. Lots of
    housing (1,500 beds) within 10 miles of area.
How to Get There: I–91 north to Exit 3 at Brattleboro, Ver-

mont; then Route 9E to junction of Route 63; south on Route 63 to center of Chesterfield; turn left for 1 mile to Jackson Hill Road; follow to the touring center.

Here is a Revolutionary War farmstead in the gently rolling landscape near Mt. Monadnock that has served as equestrian land for nearly thirty years. Ezra Jackson was a homsteader on this 600-acre tract in 1778. At first snowfall the bridle paths are instantly transformed into cross-country trails that are well conceived and cared for. The ski terrain varies from open meadows to deep wooded forests and sudden clearings that look out over the Green Mountains of southern Vermont: Monadnock, Ascutney, Stratton, Bromley, Haystack, Snow, and Lake Spofford—a 40-mile vista. After the 30 kilometers are exhausted—rather impossible even in a season of regular visits—skiers can access the large forests of the 12,000-acre Pisgah Wilderness Area, a region where ungroomed logging trails and paths course endlessly. Rentals are available at Road's End Farm, as well as informal instruction by appointment.

THE DARBY FIELD INN
Box D, Bald Hill
Conway, New Hampshire 03818
(603) 447–2181

Hours: 8 A.M. to 4 P.M.; for guests of the inn only.
Trail System: 15 kilometers (about 9 miles).
Trail Difficulty: Easiest, more difficult, most difficult.
Trail Grooming: Yes.
Rental Equipment: No.
Instruction: No.
Food Facilities: Dining room for breakfast and dinner. Dinner open to public.
Lodging: Seventeen rooms in the inn.
How to Get There: I–93 to Exit 24; Route 3 north to Route 25, northeast to Route 16; north to Bald Hill.
The top of Bald Hill provides an eagle's eye panorama of the Mountain Washington Valley and the whole Presidential Range. The scenery is as stunning as any you'll find in New

England ski country, and the setting is an inn converted from a big farmhouse—now offering seventeen bedrooms. From quaint Victorian interiors to the breadth of the New Hampshire mountain sky, the Darby Field Inn is a good choice for nearly any touring skier. After a day of tough running or just leisurely plodding through woods, the sunset view of the valley from the dining room is an amazing delight.

The trails themselves have a nice variety; they are only partially groomed and tracked and draw skiers through hilly, wooded terrain. Skiers wanting more terrain can easily jump into the White Mountain National Forest, less than 1 mile from the takeoff point at the inn. Equipment rentals, instruction, waxing advice, and the like are not available at the inn, but the ski town of North Conway is just a few miles away.

THE BALSAMS WILDERNESS
Dixville Notch, New Hampshire 03576
(603) 255–3400 or (800) 255–0600 (continental U.S.)
or (800) 255–0800 (N.H.)

Hours: 8:30 A.M. to 4 P.M.
Trail System: 60 kilometers (36 miles).
Trail Difficulty: Easiest, more difficult, most difficult.
Trail Grooming: Double trackset by machine, skating.
Rental Equipment: Cross-country and Telemark. Some skating.
Instruction: Yes.
Food Facilities: Dining at the Balsams. Cafeteria at ski area.
Lodging: More than 230 rooms in the Grand Balsams Resort Hotel.
How to Get There: I–93 to Lincoln, New Hampshire; Route 3 to Colebrook, and east on Route 26 to Dixville Notch. Alternate route from Boston: I–95 to Portsmouth; Route 16 to Route 26; west to Dixville Notch.

As a downhill area, the Balsams Wilderness "estate" has gained a reputation as one of the most pampering ski experiences in New England, and that holds for cross-country aficionados as well. Elsewhere, we have discussed the advantages of a cross-country area that can share the amenities and atmosphere of an

established downhill area on the same premises—restaurants, lodges, housing, and the trail system, to name a few. For diners the gourmet experience at the Balsams is not one to be taken lightly, no matter what your ski preference. The Grand Balsams Resort Hotel has more than 230 rooms, and the management does not care if your skis are skinny, wide, or a little of each. Rental and retail gear is available for both Alpine and Nordic.

That said, the touring experience can certainly stand on its own merits here.The trail system is set in the fortress wall of the White Mountains entrance of Dixville Notch. There is wonderful scenic wilderness throughout the region, both on the well-groomed trackset trails and the outback wilderness trails that meander across the estate.

VALLEY VIEW COUNTRY CLUB
The Taylors
Country Club Drive, Route 13
Dunbarton, New Hampshire 03045
(603) 774–5031

Hours: 9 A.M. to dusk.
Trail System: 22 kilometers (about 14 miles).
Trail Difficulty: Easiest, more difficult.
Trail Grooming: Yes; tracks with skating lanes.
Rental Equipment: Yes.
Instruction: Yes.
Food Facilities: Restaurant at the clubhouse.
Lodging: Several inns and motels within 8 miles of the center.
How to Get There: I–93 to Route 101; turn onto Route 114 in
    Goffstown and follow Route 13 North for 5½ miles to the
    country club.

Valley View Country Club is a fine example of good ski touring on golf-course terrain and surrounding countryside. It is a day-tripper's area, encompassing open-field, trackset skiing with some off-the-trail powder-breaking as well. This area operates at a leisurely pace, and novices can benefit in a low-pressure environment from a good instruction and gentle terrain. The trails around the pond are open and wooded.

125

MOOSE MOUNTAIN LODGE
Etna, New Hampshire 03750
(603) 643-3529

Hours: Daylight.
Trail System: 32 kilometers (20 miles); for guests only.
Trail Difficulty: Easiest, more difficult, most difficult.
Trail Grooming: No.
Rental Equipment: Yes, for guests.
Instruction: Informal teaching is included with the lodge stay.
Food Facilities: For guests only, three meals daily.
Lodging: Twelve guest rooms.
How to Get There: I-89 to Exit 18; Route 120 north for ½ mile to a right turn on Etna Road; turn right again ½ mile beyond the Etna Store onto Rudsboro Road; then 2 miles to a left turn onto Dana Road. Go ½ mile, then turn right up hill. Caution: At times this is tricky terrain to negotiate by car. Please call ahead.

Once an Alpine area in the formative days of the sport (the 1930s), Moose Mountain was converted into a ski-touring center that commands the lovely sweep of the Green Mountains and the Connecticut River Valley. Ghosts of those pioneer skiers seem still with the place, though now Kay and Peter Shumway operate the area solely as an inn, with ski touring a feature attraction for guests only. The area lacks public facilities, and at times the steep ascent up Moose Mountain is accessible only to overland vehicles. The area features a trail system that begins uphill at the front door of the inn. Skiers skim quickly into the fir woodlands and then run down through exhilarating chutes out into dazzling open meadows. Here, the Appalachian Trail crosses, and skiers can use the many trails established by the Dartmouth Outing Club. The interior of the lodge is ideal for folks who have long since traded in the crowded nightlife for lingering home-cooked meals in front of radiant stone fireplaces.

TORY PINES
Route 47
Francestown, New Hampshire 03043
(603) 588-2000

Hours: 9 A.M. to 4:30 P.M.
Trail System: 13 kilometers (about 8 miles); combined with
   Crotched Mountain trails.
Trail Difficulty: Easiest, more difficult, most difficult.
Trail Grooming: Daily.
Rental Equipment: 100 sets.
Instruction: Yes.
Food Facilities: Restaurant in the center of trail system.
Lodging: Twenty-eight rooms in the hotel; another hotel ¹⁄₁₀
   mile away.
How to Get There: Take I–91 to Brattleboro, Vermont; Route 9
   east to Keene, New Hampshire; Route 101 east to Route
   202; north on Route 202 to Route 47 and then east to Tory
   Pines.

Tory Pines combined efforts with Crotched Mountain to operate a 50-kilometer groomed, trackset, marked, and patrolled
trail system. This boosts the Tory Pine traditional system by
about 20 kilometers and opens the ski terrain into some hilly
challenges and real cruising destinations for lunchtime stops.
The areas combine their efforts also on the purchase of rental
equipment, retail gear, and instruction—including Telemarking, which makes use of Crotched's downhill slopes. There is
special attention here to beginners, who can purchase attractive
lesson/rental/trail-pass packages. Night skiing and Alpine are
also available.
   Tory itself is a 400-acre spread at the foot of Crotched and
offers skiing over open golf-course terrain and through dense
woods that open suddenly into spectacular views of the Monadnock region of lakes and mountains. All trails seem to lead
eventually to a wonderful Revolutionary-period tavern, the
Snooty Fox, that features fireside wine sipping and gourmet
cuisine.

CANNON MOUNTAIN
Franconia, New Hampshire 03580
(603) 823–5563

Hours: 8 A.M. to 4:30 P.M., at Alpine area with access to cross-country trails.
Trail System: 8 kilometers (5 miles); bike paths good for skiing when snow-covered.
Trail Difficulty: Easiest, more difficult.
Trail Grooming: None.
Rental Equipment: Yes, in nearby shop.
Instruction: No.
Food Facilities: Restaurants nearby; a snack bar and cafeteria at the mountain.
Lodging: Motels and inns in the region.
How to Get There: I–93 to Lincoln, then Route 3 through Franconia Notch to Exit 1, Flume Visitors' Center for bikepaths; Exit 3 for Echo Lake Parking Lot.

Cannon is one of the woolliest of the old-time ski areas. It was hewn out of the rugged granite uplands back in the skimeister days of the 1930s before disciplines were so specialized. Thus, it is possible that members of the Nansen Ski Club, the first ski-touring organization in the nation, skinned their way up Cannon and jumped off the edge of the earth for a shot down the Taft Highway. These days, of course, there is a full, small-ish, Nordic trail system as well as the Alpine area of Cannon. The Nordic area is rather casual, but pretty. Nordic skiers leave from the Echo Lake parking lot at Franconia Notch State Park and run in the woodlands at the base of these granite towers. The trail system is within the state park.

FRANCONIA INN CROSS-COUNTRY SKI AREA
Route 116, Easton Road
Franconia, New Hampshire 03580
(603) 823–5542 or 1–800–RELAXX

Hours: 9 A.M. to 5 P.M.
Trail System: 60 kilometers (about 38 miles).
Trail Difficulty: Easiest, more difficult, most difficult.
Trail Grooming: All groomed and trackset.
Rental Equipment: Yes.
Instruction: Yes.
Food Facilities: Restaurant at inn.
Lodging: Rooms available at inn.
How to Get There: I–93 to Franconia; Exit 38, Route 116 south,
    then 2½ miles to Inn on right.

Located in one of the historic mountain settings of the Northeast, this ski area offers a view of the notch, of the Kinsman
Range, of Mt. Lafayette, and the entire eastern valley of the
White Mountain Range. It is land steeped in outdoor history. It
is also quite demanding in spots, groomed with a lovely touch,
and easily accessible from Boston. The trail system itself,
spread out through the granite knobs and fir-forest-terrain of
the region, is a healthy 38 miles and ranges from gently sloped
meadows to high shoulder skiing. With the number of motels,
inns, and restaurants surrounding this trail system, it is fun to
make a loop of many days. Maps are available showing you just
how to do this.

Franconia Inn itself is a pleasant facility, and the barn beside it is a good retail shop for waxes and gear, instruction, con-
tacts with guides, and box lunches for the trail. The inn is a
fine destination for skiers who want to keep coming back.

AMC PINKHAM NOTCH CAMP
Box 298
Gorham, New Hampshire 03581
(603) 466–2725

Hours: Daylight.
Trail System: 50 kilometers (about 31 miles).
Trail Difficulty: Easiest, more difficult, most difficult.
Trail Grooming: None.
Rental Equipment: None.
Instruction: No formal program.
Food Facilities: Breakfast and dinner at base camp; reservations
   required for dinner. Trail lunches available if ordered the
   night before. Buffet lunches on weekends.
Lodging: Capacity for more than 100 persons; reservations ad-
   vised. Dormitory-style bunking; shared baths.
How to Get There: I–95 to the Spaulding Turnpike to Route 16.
   Camp is 17 miles north of North Conway.

The AMC Camp at Pinkham Notch, the base of Mt. Washington, is one of the original outback mountaineering camps in
New England. It is for the serious of purpose, the skillful, the
experienced skier. That said, Pinkham Notch Camp also provides some of the greatest wilderness skiing anywhere. In
places the trails are tied in with the Jackson Ski Touring facility, which is of similar stripe. Along with individual skiing,
there are several programs available, including weekend workshops, winter camping and snowshoeing, Telemarking, and
photography. There are also evening programs and lectures.
   Located at the eastern base of Mt. Washington in the heart
of the White Mountain National Forest, the Pinkham Camp
opens onto the rolling terrain of the shoulders of the Presidential Range, including the downhill area of Wildcat. This is some
of the most breathtaking scenery in the Northeast, and there are
several choices. One stimulating 6-miler is the Avalanche Brook
Ski Trail, connecting Pinkham Notch Camp with the Dana
Place Inn to the south. This trail climbs nearly 1,000 feet, then
drops 1,500 feet through fir and hardwood thicket. You'll cross
bridges over streams, then end with a 1-mile run over Rocky
Branch Trail and a meadow surrounding the Dana Place Inn.

This is one of the typical Pinkham Camp trails, and the most adventurous can pick up the trail from Jackson on this route. Described as "challenging skiing," that really means knowing what you're about. Don't attempt it alone or in bad skiing conditions. On the other hand, the reward of such a trail is some of the most exhilarating skiing in New England.

EASTMAN SKI TOURING CENTER
Box 53
Grantham, New Hampshire 03753
(603) 863–4500

Hours: 9 A.M. to 4 P.M.
Trail System: 30 kilometers (about 19 miles).
Trail Difficulty: Easiest, more difficult, most difficult.
Trail Grooming: Groomed and double trackset.
Rental Equipment: 95 sets.
Instruction: Group and semiprivate lessons including Telemark and skating clinics.
Food Facilities: Harvey's Restaurant at the center serves drinks and lunch.
Lodging: Inns and motels in the area.
How to Get There: I–93 to I–89 north at Bow, New Hampshire, to Exit 13 at Grantham; turn right; the Eastman road is less than a ½ mile on the right.

Eastman is a lovely four-season vacation resort spread out in the pine valley of the Sugar River in the west-central region of the state. The well-marked and -cared for trail system encompasses all the features of the resort: golf course, woods, rolling hills including a small Alpine slope, and stream beds that feed into Eastman Pond. Novice skiers can work on the relative flats of Lazy Loop around the golf course, and as they get adventurous, work out into the woods loops. The 5-kilometer Deerpath Loop will test anyone's skills, and for distance, skirting Eastman Pond can be close to a 9-kilometer project. The countryside is pretty, with views of the surrounding mountains, and the amenities at the center are complete: rental and retail shop, waxing area, and ready instruction. At the center, Harvey's is a good-sized lounge that serves drinks and a limited lunch menu.

INTERVALE NORDIC SKI TOURING CENTER
Intervale, New Hampshire 03845
800–282–5220

Hours: 9 A.M. to 5 P.M., December 1 to March 30.
Trail System: 35 kilometers (about 22 miles) of groomed trail with 70 kilometers (about 43 miles) overall.
Trail Difficulty: Easiest, more difficult, most difficult.
Trail Grooming: Trackset over 60 kilometers.
Rental Equipment: 200 sets.
Instruction: PSIA-certified ski school.
Food Facilities: Several nearby restaurants and three inns.
Lodging: Country inns and motor lodges.
How to Get There: I–93 to Exit 24; Route 3 north to Route 25; northeast to Route 16, north through Conway and North Conway; then Route 16A 3 miles to the center.

Located in the Mt. Washington Valley, the Intervale Ski Touring Center is dedicated to the proposition that skiers at any level can learn a thing or twenty about the sport. The instructors are as fun as they are effective and will eventually want to work you out on the hillside. The trails are well marked and groomed, most of them offering nice views of Mt. Washington and the Moat Range. Skiers will use many of the old logging roads that crisscross the region, and some may opt to climb the saddle of Bartlett Mountain with its scenic overlooks. Several moonlight and cookout tours are available through the season.

JACKSON SKI TOURING FOUNDATION
Box 2160
Jackson, New Hampshire 03846
(603) 383–9355

Hours: 8 A.M. to 5:30 P.M.
Trail System: 160 kilometers (103 miles).
Trail Difficulty: Easiest, more difficult, most difficult.
Trail Grooming: 60 kilometers groomed daily; 45 kilometers for skating.

Rental Equipment: Yes.
Instruction: Yes.
Food Facilities: Several nearby restaurants.
Lodging: Several inns and motels in the area.
How to Get There: I-95 to Spaulding Turnpike; Route 16N to
    Jackson; center is in middle of village.

Aside from its legendary stature as the historic capital of cross-
country skiing, and with plenty of echoes of the skimeister
days when it took all morning to "skin" up Black Mountain for
one run down, the village of Jackson is simply astoundingly
beautiful. Classic New England is what you get here, from the
old covered bridge that welcomes you into town to the white
church in the center of the village, and the exciting pace of serious ski touring—all under the command of Mt. Washington.

Do not be deterred by the talk of serious skiing, however.
True, from start to finish Jackson exudes the sport. But still,
there's plenty here for the novice, the snowshoer, the hiker, or
the vacationer simply looking for delicious mountain experience.

Jackson truly goes to the roots of the region. It is a nonprofit operation that combines the efforts of the U.S. Forest Ser-

vice and several private landowners. Since the 1970s it has been incorporated for the sole purpose of advancing cross-country skiing. Of the 152 kilometers of trails, 60 are groomed carefully, and often. Skiers wind through hardwood forest land, open-gladed meadows, and upland wilderness that leads into the shoulders of the Presidential Range. Across the river and into the trees, the Ellis River Trail winds in a long, slightly uphill loop along the river to a woodland inn; the way home is an easy downhill breezer all the way back to the road. For off-track skiers there is ample opportunity for backpacking and camping trips into the backlands on mountain skis.

At the Jackson Ski Touring Foundation building you will find the Jack Frost Ski Shop, which will rent or sell equipment and all kinds of retail accessories. Here you can sign up for a lesson, taking a waxing clinic, or sign up for a night-skiing foray. And, finally, for the inexhaustible, Jackson and its environs has a full lineup of terrific nightlife.

SHATTUCK INN NORDIC SKI CENTER
Jaffrey, New Hampshire 03452
(603) 532–4300

Hours: 9 A.M. to 4:30 P.M.
Trail System: 13 kilometers (about 9 miles).
Trail Difficulty: Easiest, more difficult.
Trail Grooming: All groomed and trackset.
Rental Equipment: Yes.
Instruction: No.
Food Facilities: Snack bar.
Lodging: Inns in the area.
How to Get There: From Nashua take Route 101 west to Peterboro, then south on Route 202 to Jaffrey Center.

When the winter sends southern New Hampshire her fair share of snowfall, Shattuck becomes one of those golf course ski areas that gets transformed into deep winter. On the course itself, the skiing is confined to the cart paths that branch throughout the eighteen holes. This is lovely skiing at the base of Mt. Monadnock.

WOODBOUND INN
Jaffrey, New Hampshire 03452
(603) 532–8341

Hours: 9 A.M. to 5 P.M.
Trail System: 36 kilometers (about 22 miles).
Trail Difficulty: Easiest, more difficult, most difficult.
Trail Grooming: As needed.
Rental Equipment: Yes.
Instruction: Yes.
Food Facilities: Restaurant at the inn, serving all three meals.
Lodging: Forty-two rooms and cottages at the inn.
How to Get There: Route 2 in Massachusetts to Route 202, then north into New Hampshire and to Woodbound.

With 36 kilometers of nicely set tracks opening into the state forest land—not to mention a downhill practice slope for Telemark work—Woodbound has a total ski experience to offer its guest. The trail system varies from gently rolling flattish land, with running tracks, to wilderness shots up, down, and all around through the public lands.

In addition, Woodbound offers the extras for everyone to enjoy all the little corners of winter—from night tobogganing down specially sculpted chutes, to ice skating and sleigh rides, then indoors for movies. The food is homemade and renowned in ski country.

GUNSTOCK CROSS-COUNTRY CENTER
Box 1307
Laconia, New Hampshire 03247
(603) 293–4341

Hours: 8:30 A.M. to 4 P.M.
Trail System: 32 kilometers (about 21 miles).
Trail Difficulty: Easiest, more difficult, most difficult.
Trail Grooming: Double trackset daily, skating lanes.
Rental Equipment: 100 sets.
Instruction: All ability levels, including Telemark.

Food Facilities: Cafeteria in the main ski lodge; soup, sandwiches, and snacks.
Lodging: Several motels and inns nearby.
How to Get There: I-93 to Exit 20; Route 3 to Route 11A; follow to Gunstock.

With its 5-kilometer zinger, where several U.S. Nordic Combined championships have been held, to its gentle trails that wind the novice skier through some lovely winter woods, Gunstock offers the entire spectrum of the sport. And as with many Alpine-Nordic combinations, cross-country skiing here shares the amenities of the well-established downhill facility. Yet, there is a rustic Touring Center that seems built around a huge wood stove and offers Nordic aficionados everything they will want or need. The intermediate trails are pretty and varied. Skiing begins on farm fields sectioned by ancient stone walls, then proceeds to brookside trails that run through cathedral-like stands of pine and birch forest. There is plenty of touring off the trail as well, leading experts up the flank of Mt. Cobble and into the notch between Cobble and Gunstock. From the high terrain you overlook Lake Winnipesaukee. From here, for the hearty, there is a 3-mile racing loop that skirts Cobble and returns to the hospitable base lodge.

LOON MOUNTAIN CROSS-COUNTRY CENTER
Route 112, Loon Mountain Road
Lincoln, New Hampshire 03251
(603) 745–8111, Extension 568

Hours: 8 A.M. to 5 P.M.
Trail System: 35 kilometers (about 23 miles).
Trail Difficulty: Easiest, more difficult, most difficult.
Trail Grooming: Daily; skate-groomed and trackset.
Rental Equipment: Yes.
Instruction: Yes; PSIA-certified.
Food Facilities: Lunches available at the base lodge.
Lodging: A forty-unit inn at the mountain, as well as several rental condominiums through the Loon reservation service.

How to Get There: I–93 to Exit 32; Route 112 east in New Hampshire, then Loon Mountain Road.

Though touring at this popular Alpine area has all the advantages and drawbacks that go along with sharing facilities with downhill types, the Loon trails lead you quickly into the wilderness of the Pemigewasset National Forest. Skiing here follows a spider web of old logging roads and deer paths, with sudden views of the Franconia Range of the White Mountains. Trails course through the deep solitude of snow-impacted stream beds and slab up the sides of steep hills in spots. They are well marked. The trail system also employs the Alpine slopes for you to go out on your Telemark skinny skis and show the jellybeans what real skiing is. The nightlife at Loon holds countless opportunities for the tireless.

PERRY HOLLOW CROSS-COUNTRY CENTER
New Durham, New Hampshire 03894
(603) 569–3055

Hours: 8:30 A.M. to 4:30 P.M.
Trail System: 25 kilometers (about 15 miles).
Trail Difficulty: Easiest, more difficult, most difficult.
Trail Grooming: All groomed; 15 kilometers trackset; 5 kilometers skating.
Rental Equipment: Yes.
Instruction: Ski school; group lessons.
Food Facilities: Snacks available.
Lodging: Inns and motels in the area.
How to Get There: From Route 95 at Portsmouth take Spaulding Turnpike to Rochester, then follow Route 11 to New Durham.

Perry Hollow is a broad trail system that allows for all kinds of skiing, from the traditional tours in the woods to high-speed skating on a five-kilometer track. The area is located in the easy-to-reach region of southern New Hampshire near the lower reaches of Winnipesaukee. When the snow is right, the skiing is excellent with room enough for all tastes.

WINDBLOWN SKI TOURING
RFD 2, Box 669
New Ipswich, New Hampshire 03071
(603) 878–2869

Hours: 9 A.M. to 5 P.M.
Trail System: 30 kilometers (about 19 miles).
Trail Difficulty: Easiest, more difficult, most difficult.
Trail Grooming: 15 kilometers groomed daily; skating lanes. Some night skiing.
Rental Equipment: 125 sets.
Instruction: Weekends; by appointment on weekdays.
Food Facilities: Soup and sandwiches available.
Lodging: Inns and motels in the area. Warming hut available overnight by arrangement; sleeps twelve.
How to Get There: Route 2 west to Leomenster, Exit at Route 13 north, follow into Townsend; head west on Route 119. Turn right at sign for New Ipswich, Route 124. Facility is 11 miles up on left.

This high-elevation touring center in the sweeping Monadnock countryside usually has a long season, pushing well into April most years. It is a full-amenity center with a good base lodge complete with rentals, retail shop, waxing room, and a simple hearty kitchen for trail's end when skiers kick their feet up in front of the radiant wood stove. Deep in the middle of the 19-mile trail system there is a warming hut in the woods for ski-hikers to lay out a bedroll for the night or for day skiers to stop for lunch. There are three other shelters in the woods as well.

NORSK CROSS-COUNTRY SKI CENTER
Route 11, Box 735
New London, New Hampshire 03257
(603) 526–4685

Hours: 9 A.M. to 5 P.M.
Trail System: 90 kilometers (55 miles).
Trail Difficulty: Easiest, more difficult, most difficult.
Trail Grooming: Groomed and trackset.

Rental Equipment: 150 sets.
Instruction: Classes at 10:30 A.M., noon, and 1 P.M., by arrangment.
Food Facilities: Restaurant and lounge on premises.
Lodging: Inn on the premises. Separate phone: (603) 526–6040.
How to Get There: I–93 to I–89 to Exit 11; east 1½ miles past Grey House Restaurant to the first right-hand turn.

This touring center on the skirts of Mt. Kearsarge offers some excellent large and varied terrain for touring in the region. All trails are well groomed and well marked; the loops are intelligently conceived, both for novice skiers looking for their first short loop and for experts who want to run a marathon through these foothills. One of the nicest features is that Norsk is a major-sized area just two hours from Boston near Sunapee and King Ridge—two Alpine areas made for Nordic whizzes who are ready to try out their Telemark technique. Norsk has a full spate of services, including rentals, retail gear, food, and lodging at the nice, white-gabled Lake Sunapee Country Club and Inn. Excellent maps are available, as are special events—from moonlight tours to sauna tours to racing, skating, and Telemark workshops.

DEER CAP SKI TOURING CENTER
Route 16
Ossipee, New Hampshire 03814
(603) 539–6030

Hours: 8:30 A.M. to 4:30 P.M.
Trail System: 20 kilometers (about 13 miles).
Trail Difficulty: Easiest, more difficult, most difficult.
Trail Grooming: Groomed and trackset as needed.
Rental Equipment: 100 sets.
Instruction: By appointment only.
Food Facilities: Trail snacks at the center.
Lodging: Inns and motels in the area within 2 miles.
How to Get There: I–95 to Portsmouth, New Hampshire; Spaulding Turnpike to Route 16 north to Center Ossipee.

Think you're a hotshot? Think you can bring a little place like Deer Cap to its knees with your dazzle? Then the Superstar trail is for you. Deer Cap may not have much expert terrain, but this windy, snaggy heart-stopper will be taken seriously by skiers on every level since it is one of the toughest you can find. Most of the trails here wind through pretty, fairly flat terrain in pine woods. The lodge has an eating center with a snack bar, rest rooms, and plenty of room to wax your skis. The trails begin just outside the door.

TEMPLE MOUNTAIN SKI TOURING
Route 101, Box 368
Peterborough, New Hampshire 03458
(603) 924–6949

Hours: 9 A.M. to 4:30 P.M.
Trail System: 43 kilometers (about 26 miles).
Trail Difficulty: Easiest, more difficult, most difficult.
Trail Grooming: 8 kilometers groomed, 6 of them trackset. Some skating lanes.
Rental Equipment: More than 100 sets.
Instruction: Yes, both weekdays and weekends. Check the schedule.
Food Facilities: Cafeteria and lounge in the main lodge.
Lodging: None on the mountain; several hotels, motels, and inns in the region.
How to Get There: Route 3 north to Nashua; Route 101A to 101 West to Peterborough to Temple Mountain.

Several improvements have changed this already excellent and well-appointed ski-touring area. Many of the trails have been widened and improved, with new terrain being opened all the time. More and more of the terrain is being tracked, and a new Telemark program has been designed, making use of the broad downhill trails on Temple.

At an elevation between 1,500 and 2,000 feet, Temple usually records an annual snowfall of between 10 and 14 feet and is a paradise for powderhounds no matter what they have on their feet. Add to this much snow the fact that Temple is less than 70 miles from Boston, and you have the makings of a major ski-touring area for the snow-starved folks from New England's flatlands.

The skiing, which combines its own large system with the 20-mile Wapack Trail, takes tourers across fir-ringed mountain ridges with sudden dramatic overlooks; then the trail may plunge down across meadowland into hardwood groves and stream beds. For the adventurous, narrower trails wind off the beaten path through thickets of snow-heavy evergreen boughs and lead skiers into day-long wilderness tours. There are several shelters scattered throughout the trail system. The area also provides a full variety of skier services. Cafeteria-style food is available in the lodge.

SNOWVILLAGE INN
Snowville, New Hampshire 03849
(603) 447–2818

Hours: 9 A.M. to 4 P.M. For guests only.
Trail System: 13 kilometers (about 8 miles); downhill ski trails also available nearby.
Trail Difficulty: Easiest, more difficult, most difficult.
Trail Grooming: Some; limited skating.
Rental Equipment: Yes.
Instruction: Weekends, or weekdays by appointment.
Food Facilities: Full meals and bar available at Snowvillage Inn.
Lodging: Snowvillage Inn, plus inns and motels throughout the Mount Washington Valley. Child care by reservation.
How to Get There: I–95 to Spaulding Turnpike to Route 16 north to Conway; Route 153 to sign for Snowville and Brownfield; at Snowville, right on Foss Mountain Road.

With good reason, the Snowvillage Inn, an Edwardian estate in the lap of Mt. Washington, 1,100 feet high in its foothills, has gained the reputation as one of the most spectacular winter vacation spots in the region. Though only 6 miles out of Conway, the inn is secluded in the upper woodlands of Foss Mountain; from the porch guests have a sweeping panoramic view of the valley, with Mt. Washington itself looming over the place, close enough to touch, it seems.

The skiing is of the woodland variety with groomed and trackset trails (150 acres) that take skiers into thickets and out again for sudden high-altitude overviews of the valley. The skiing is lovely, convenient, and thoroughly accommodated to tourers. But it is the inn that cuts Snowvillage above the ordinary. With its 19 cozy bedrooms, and the crackling fire in a big country living room cluttered with books, magazines, and dozing dogs, this inn is as honestly homey and convivial as they come. In the dining room guests are served multicourse gourmet meals, beginning, perhaps, with Hungarian mushroom soup and ending with Cognac back at the fire. It is difficult to exaggerate the elegance and charm of the Snowvillage Inn in its après-ski mode.

SUNSET HILL TOURING CENTER
Sugar Hill, New Hampshire 03585
(603) 823–5522

Hours: 8 A.M. to dusk.
Trail System: 60 kilometers (about 40 miles).
Trail Difficulty: Easiest, more difficult, most difficult.
Trail Grooming: 15 kilometers groomed daily; some skating.
Rental Equipment: 100 sets.
Instruction: Yes.
Food Facilities: Soup is served at the touring center; full meals at the inn.
Lodging: Thirty-five rooms at the inn.
How to Get There: I–93 to Franconia; Route 117 west to Sunset Hill.

Atop Sugar Hill in the White Mountains sits the Sunset House, an old New England inn with nice flavor of its own and excellent, nearly limitless skiing possibilities. Its own trails run into the Franconia Inn network, as well as a few other trail systems in this well-toured region. Skiers can slide all day over the lower flats of the valley or chug up through the timber-ringed upper plateaus for an overview of the impressive geography of the region. Back at the Sunset Hill Center, skiers like to hang out at the ski shop with its kettle of homemade soup simmer-

ing on the stove. All the amenities are available, from instruction to rental and retail equipment. This is also the place to
sign up for guided day and moonlight tours. The inn has a fine
restaurant for food and drink; it offers high-quality lodging.

THE INN AT EAST HILL FARM
Troy, New Hampshire 03465
(603) 242-6495

Hours: Daylight.
Trail System: 20 kilometers (about 13 miles).
Trail Difficulty: Easiest, more difficult, most difficult.
Trail Grooming: As needed. Trackset.
Rental Equipment: 130 sets.
Instruction: Yes.
Food Facilities: Full restaurant at the inn, serving breakfast,
    lunch, and dinner.
Lodging: Cottages available; rooms at the inn.
How to Get There: I-91 to Brattleboro, Vermont; Route 9 east
    to Keene, New Hampshire; Route 12 south to Troy; left on
    Jaffrey Road to the inn.

East Hill Farm is one of those country inns that, while not
monumental in size and scope, does many things with excel-
lence. Most notably, all the terrain here is gentle and appealing,
with its lovely scenery around the base of Mt. Monadnock. The
farm itself is also appealing, producing delicious country-style
meals and offering indoor swimming, sauna, and a skating rink.
East Hill Farm is a complete and well-appointed touring destination.

WATERVILLE VALLEY CROSS-COUNTRY SKI AREA
Waterville Valley, New Hampshire 03215
(603) 236–4666

Hours: 9 am. to 4:30 P.M., all week.
Trail System: 70 kilometers (about 45 miles).
Trail Difficulty: Easiest, more difficult, most difficult.
Trail Grooming: Yes; both traditional trackset and skating lanes.
Rental Equipment: Yes.
Instruction: PSIA-certified.
Food Facilities: Finish Line Restaurant at the Touring Center.
Lodging: Several inns and rental condominiums.
How to Get There: I–93 north to Exit 28; Route 49 east to Waterville Valley.

Waterville Valley is one of the major Alpine ski centers in the Northeast and in recent years has become a self-contained ski village for all sizes, styles, and levels of the sport. Using all the meadows and woods in the region, cross-country buffs have nearly unlimited touring. On the more organized trail system, skiers will follow miles of old logging roads, starting from a cluster of rustic buildings that comprise the center. The trail web rolls outward from this spot, a carefully graded, marked, and groomed system. Some trails roll through gentle woodland flats, while others mount precipitously toward high-country plateaus and nice vistas of the surrounding mountains. Alpine and Nordic forms mix at Waterville when it is time for coaches at the school to give Telemark instruction. The teaching also features demonstrations, workshops of all kinds, and video teaching. For beginners, there is a fine special "starter kit" to get you rolling with a day of free rentals and no trail fee. Look for a full complement of rental and retail goods, and ask about the race program. This is a world-class ski area with many top-shelf events in its list of credits. For those who like nightlife and/or elegant dining, there are some good bars and restaurants in the village. Most skiing and social life is centered around the new Town Square village center.

THE NORDIC SKIER
19 North Main Street
Wolfeboro, New Hampshire 03894
(603) 569–3151

Hours: 9 A.M. to 5:30 P.M.
Trail System: 40 kilometers (about 26 miles).
Trail Difficulty: Easiest, more difficult, most difficult.
Trail Grooming: Yes; trackset with 7 kilometers of skating
    lanes.
Rental Equipment: 100 sets.
Instruction: PSIA-certified.
Food Facilities: In the town and area.
Lodging: In the town and area.
How to Get There: I–93N to Exit Route 3; north to Route 28
    North to Wolfeboro.

Wolfeboro is a fishing town. Summer and winter, the folks talk
fishing, anticipate it, clean up after it, and get ready for more.
Yet there is a certain season after the first snow falls in November, when another kind of sportsman comes into Wolfeboro—
the touring skier. Along with snowmobilers and ice fishermen,
the town also becomes the cross-country center of the Lakes
Region. There are two separate trail systems that offer a variety
of experiences (though without the real toe-curling black terrain)—the more challenging Abenaki Trails, and the Lakeview
network for novice or easy skiing. There are also plenty of
woods, unplowed logging roads, and wilderness skiing for off-
track aficionados. There is a good touring specialty shop at
hand in Wolfeboro as the town has come to cater to skiers.
Rentals, guides, retail gear, instruction, and all sorts of moonlight skiing and workshops are available here as well. Good
food and lodging abound in wide variety.

146

MAINE

20.

17.

13.

12.

5.

6.

19. 15.

11.

10.

21. 14.

4.

16.

2.

7. 18.

1.

3.

9. 8.

95

N.

Maine

Numbers on map refer to towns numbered below.

1. Auburn, *Snorada Recreation Center* 150
2. Augusta, *Natanis Cross-Country Ski Trails* 150
3. Bar Harbor, *Acadia National Park* 151
4. Bethel, *Bethel Inn Ski Touring Center* 152
    Carter's Cross-Country Ski Area 153
    Sunday River Cross-Country Ski Center 154
5. Brownville, *Little Lyford Pond Lodge* 155
6. Carrabassett Valley, *Carrabassett Valley Recreation Center* . 157
7. Center Lovell, *Westways on Kezar Lake* 158
8. Cumberland, *Val Halla Country Club*
    and Cross-Country Ski Center 159
9. Dayton, *Harris Farm Stand Ski Touring* 159
10. Dixmont, *Ben-Loch Farm Ski Touring Center* 160
11. Farmington, *Holley Farm Resort* 161
    Titcomb Mountain Ski Touring Center 162
    Troll Valley Cross-Country Center 163
12. The Forks, *Crab Apple Inn* 164
13. Greenville, *Chesuncook Lake House* 165
    Mountain View Farm Cross-Country Ski Center 166
14. Jay, *Spruce Mountain Cross-Country Center* 167
15. Kingfield, *Winter's Inn Ski Touring Center* 168
16. Locke Mills, *Mount Abram Ski Touring* 169
17. Millinocket, *Baxter State Park* 169
    Katahdin Lake Wilderness Camps 171
18. Oxford, *Carter's Farm Market Ski Touring Center* 172
19. Rangeley, *Saddleback* 173
20. Rockwood, *The Birches Ski Touring Center* 174
21. Rumford, *Black Mountain of Maine* 176

SNORADA RECREATION CENTER
525 Lake Street
Auburn, Maine 04210
(207) 748–0191

Hours: Monday through Friday, 11 A.M. to 9 P.M.; weekends, 9
A.M. to 9 P.M. (Night skiing on a lighted trail loop.)
Trail System: 15 kilometers (about 10 miles); groomed, track-
set, skating lanes. Some wilderness.
Trail Difficulty: Easiest, more difficult, most difficult.
Trail Grooming: Groomed and trackset.
Rental Equipment: Yes.
Instruction: Lessons by appointment.
Food Facilities: Snack bar at center; full restaurants within ½
mile of the center.
Lodging: In Auburn.
How to Get There: Maine Turnpike to Exit 12 in Auburn; after
tolls take a left on Washington Avenue and follow down-
town through three sets of lights. Left on Court Street and
bear right onto lake Street; the center is about 2 miles up
Lake Street.

This cosmopolitan touring center is the site of the Bates College Winter Carnival and plenty of citizen racing, including a
Bill Koch League and Tuesday-night races that give it a rather
vigorous cast. The terrain varies from open field to some woods
running loops, over two somewhat challenging ridges and
across a frozen lake. It is fine touring, and there are plans to ex-
pand the trail system. The center has rental and retail equipment and provides a waxing room and trail snacks.

NATANIS CROSS-COUNTRY SKI TRAILS
RFD 1, Box 554
Augusta, Maine 04330
(207) 622–6533

Hours: December 26 to March 1, Monday to Friday, 9 A.M. to
dark; weekends, dawn to dusk.
Trail System: 10 kilometers (about 6 miles).

Trail Difficulty: Easiest, more difficult.
Trail Grooming: Trackset, skating.
Rental Equipment: Yes.
Instruction: For beginners.
Food Facilities: Trail snacks available at the center; full restaurant meals within 4 miles.
Lodging: Motel within 4 miles.
How to Get There: Maine Turnpike to Augusta, then Route 201 north. After passing Cony High School in Augusta, the center is 8 miles on Route 201.

Beginning with open field warm-ups, the Natanis trails take skiers through deep forest where, despite the proximity to the city, an abundance of wildlife makes its presence known. You'll see signs of moose, deer, rabbit, and fox as you ski over this rolling terrain. One trail leads out to a beaver bog, where the animals have felled trees to build their lodges to hibernate the winter away. Not a heavy challenge for the mountain-man skier, Natanis is nevertheless a pretty, well-run ski area. Town-sponsored citizen races and moonlight tours are part of the fun here.

ACADIA NATIONAL PARK
Box 177
Bar Harbor, Maine 04609
(207) 288–3338

Hours: 24 hours a day; headquarters, 8:30 A.M. to 4:30 P.M.
Trail System: 79 kilometers (about 49 miles) for ski touring and snowshoeing only.
Trail Difficulty: Easiest, more difficult.
Trail Grooming: None.
Rental Equipment: Ski shops in the area.
Instruction: None.
Food Facilities: Nearby.
Lodging: Nearby.
How to Get There: Maine Turnpike to Route 3, follow through Ellsworth to Bar Harbor; right on Route 233 for 3 miles to park headquarters.

151

Acadia National Park is one of the splendid natural wonders of
New England and a longstanding attraction for millions of
summertime visitors. In winter, however, this coastal forest
with its glimpses of the stormy, rock-bound coast and the
steady sea roar is quite a moving experience for most skiers.
Nature can overwhelm you here just a bit, and you return, even
from a three-hour trip, feeling you have been far away for a long
time. The park authority has done a good job separating the ski-
trail system from snowmobiles—and giving skiers nearly 50
miles to themselves. The trail loops are built over the wide,
gravel-packed carriage roads. Though ungroomed, most are
trackset by previous skiers.

There are loops of just an hour or two, or routes that incorporate a day's skiing through the snow-laden woods, over ice-
crusted, gurgling brooks, and into places like Eagle Lake and
Jordan Pond. One route takes skiers nearly across to Somes
Sound and Northeast Harbor at the seaward end of the pen-
nisula—Maine's Motif Number One. For day skiers who pack a
trail lunch and take off, good trail maps are available at the
ranger station. Toilet facilities are available near Eagle Lake.

BETHEL INN SKI TOURING CENTER
P.O. Box 49
Bethel, Maine 04217
(207) 824–2175

Hours: 8 A.M. to 5 P.M.
Trail System: 25 kilometers (about 16 miles).
Trail Difficulty: Easiest, more difficult, most difficult.
Trail Grooming: Yes, on all terrain; skating on 15 kilometers.
Rental Equipment: Yes.
Instruction: Group and private lessons daily, including Tele-
    marking.
Food Facilities: Main dining room or library open for breakfast
    and dinner; soups and sandwiches available in the tavern at
    lunchtime.
Lodging: At the inn.
How to Get There: Maine Turnpike to Exit 11; Route 26 north
    into Bethel.

The Bethel Inn hardly needs an introduction to aficionados of the rural Northeast. It is a New England classic, its stately colonial yellow dominating the twin-spired Bethel Common. The entire area is a National Historic District. In summer the inn is a plush country club, in winter a first-rate ski-touring center nestled in the foothills of the White Mountains. Skiers begin right out the back door of the inn, warm up on the golf course, then plunge into the wide, well-marked wooded trails that cross frozen streams and then open into sudden panoramic views of the Longfellow Range. Most trails are made up of gently curving, undulating terrain, just right for beginners and intermediates. However, experts are invited to try their Telemarking technique on Corkscrew or the Peter Grover Hill. The latter is especially steep and good for Telemark—or Alpine—skiing.

At breakfast, skiers may purchase box lunches for the trail. Our favorite picnic tour is out to the Lake House, where skiers relax and eat in front of the big fieldstone fireplace. Après-ski is casual and friendly—piano-bar entertainment on weekends with drinks, sauna, and board games of all kinds. The inn also offers evening sleigh rides.

CARTER'S CROSS-COUNTRY SKI CENTER
Route 26
Bethel, Maine 04270
(207) 539-4848

Hours: 9 A.M. to dark.
Trail System: 70 kilometers (about 44 miles).
Trail Difficulty: Easiest, more difficult, most difficult.
Trail Grooming: Groomed and trackset when possible; skating trails available.
Rental Equipment: Yes.
Instruction: Yes.
Food Facilities: Snacks and beverages available at the site.
Lodging: Two lodge facilities with rental cabins.
How to Get There: Follow Route 95 to the Maine Turnpike. Turn off at Exit 11 and follow Route 26 north past Oxford to Bethel.

With the low-snow winters of late, Dave and Ann Carter, owners of the other Carter area in Oxford, located a second touring center in the higher country of Bethel. When there's little to no cover just 30 miles down at Oxford, the Bethel site gets plenty of natural cover. Aside from the huge, varied trail system, the Mountain Trail leads 2½-miles up the mountain, opening spectacular views of the Androscoggin River Valley. As much fun as it is to ski up the mountain, skiing back down is a rush. There's plenty of skiing here to challenge the experts, and beginners can also find lots of level ground to get their confidence in place before taking to the woods. The area has two lodging houses with ski-in cabins high up in the mountains.

SUNDAY RIVER CROSS-COUNTRY SKI CENTER
RFD 2, Box 1688
Bethel, Maine 04217
(207) 824–2410

Hours: 9 A.M. to 5 P.M.
Trail System: 40 kilometers (25 miles).
Trail Difficulty: Easiest, more difficult, most difficult.
Trail Grooming: 25 kilometers groomed and trackset; 20 kilometers of skating lanes; 10 kilometers for experts.
Rental Equipment: Yes.
Instruction: Yes.
Food Facilities: Trail snacks in the cross-country center; restaurant and lounge within ½ mile; access via road or ski trail.
Lodging: Rooms available at Sunday River Inn; sleeping bag and dormitory living also available.
How to Get There: Maine Turnpike to Exit 11 at Gray; Route 26 to Bethel, then Routes 2, 5, and 26 through Bethel to the ski-area access road; signs to the center.

Located in the beautifully wild Sunday River Valley, this cross-county center offers trails for all abilities and levels of enthusiasm. Beginners enjoy the level terrain in the pine woods near the center and soon accept the challenge of the 5-mile round trip along the valley floor to Artists' Covered Bridge. Intermediate and expert skiers appreciate the double trackset trails and have plenty of challenge with the longer, steeper trails that meander up and down the rolling hills through mixed forest growth to the trailside lean-to, the scenic overlook, and the fabled plunge known as David's Drop. The center offers night skiing by kerosene lamp on Fridays, special events throughout the winter, including the annual Sunday River 30-kilometer tour/race, and the popular season-transition triathlon, the April Fools' Day Pole, Paddle, and Paw Race, in late March. Sunday River is another of those Nordic centers that can take advantage of a well-developed Alpine area.

LITTLE LYFORD POND LODGE
Box 688
Brownville, Maine 04414
(207) 695–2821 (via radio contact)

Hours: Dawn to dusk.
Trail System: About 80 kilometers (50 miles).
Trail Difficulty: Easiest, more difficult, most difficult.
Trail Grooming: Tracked but not groomed.
Rental Equipment: None.
Instruction: Informal.
Food Facilities: Dining in the main lodge.
Lodging: Insulated cabins with wood stoves.
How to Get There: Fly-in service from Greenville, Maine.

Little Lyford is a backcountry destination area for a maximum of ten skiers. For the hearty, rather than flying in, you can ski in over a 10-kilometer trail. Daily touring is in the deep back woods of Maine's north country, over old logging roads and hardwood trails, along frozen stream beds, and over hidden ponds. Skiers will visit the spectacular Gulf Hagas Gorge and break the powder on the surrounding hillsides. The trail network varies from shorter, flatter routes to a challenging trek to the top of Elephant Mountain, or a 13-mile round-trip ski into Greenville. Also available by arrangement are custom inn-to-inn treks. After the daily touring, a sauna awaits tired bodies, and serious country dinners are served at the main lodge. Platform tennis is also available for the tireless.

CARRABASSETT VALLEY RECREATION CENTER
Box 518
Carrabassett Valley, Maine 04947
(207) 237–2205

Hours: 8:45 A.M. to 4:30 P.M.
Trail System: 85 kilometers (about 51 miles); 5 kilometers of skating lanes; 12-kilometer racing track.
Trail Difficulty: Least difficult, more difficult, most difficult.
Trail Grooming: Most trails groomed as necessary. Some wilderness skiing along the Appalachian Trail.
Rental Equipment: Yes.
Instruction: PSIA-certifed.
Food Facilities: Food served weekends and holidays.
Lodging: Inns and motels in area. Call (207) 235–2100.
How to Get There: Maine Turnpike to Exit 12 at Auburn; Route 4 to Farmington, then Route 27 toward Kingfield. The touring center is a left turn 14 miles north of Kingfield, 1 mile from Sugarloaf Mountain, an Alpine area.

This touring area (CVRA), owned by the town of Carrabassett Valley, is a groomed piece of New England's Big North Woods, and the place doesn't lose that wild feeling. Indeed, some of the excursions off the Appalachian Trail take skiers through the cedar bogs frequented by some of some of the region's large moose population. At the organized extreme, the area also takes its racing most seriously.

For novice skiers there are the wide, gently graded trails that run along the old narrow-gauge railroad bed; one favorite trail runs down along the Carrabassett River nearly to the door of the famous Red Stallion Inn. For more advanced skiers, the area has a well-marked trail system of steep verticals and descents through bogs and stream beds. The Touring Center sells good maps, provides rentals and lessons, and offers all the amenities, from hot homemade food to waxing clinics and moonlight excursions. A skating rink is also available. There is plenty of lodging available through the Sugarloaf Reservation Service at (207) 237–2861.

WESTWAYS ON KEZAR LAKE
Route 5, Box 175
Center Lovell, Maine 04016
(207) 928-2663

Hours: Daylight.
Trail System: Unlimited wilderness skiing.
Trail Difficulty: Easiest, more difficult, most difficult.
Trail Grooming: No.
Rental Equipment: No.
Instruction: No.
Food Facilities: Breakfast and dinner at the inn Wednesday to Sunday; no lunches.
Lodging: Seven guest rooms at the inn plus vacation-home rentals on premises.
How to Get There: Maine Turnpike to Route 302 west; Route 5 north for 6 miles to the inn.

Westways skiers look out for the inn at Kezar Lake, where some like to start their skiing either breaking new powder or cruising in tracks of previous skiers. This backs up to West Mountain National Forest, with its dense forest land crossed with old logging roads and paths, many of them groomed by snowmobiles. Here and there are some glimpses of the Presidential Range, as trails roll over small ponds and streams. There is open-terrain skiing for sun worshipers who prefer to stay in the rolling hills and meadows. The old stone walls and thickets contain rich wildlife throughout the grounds of this 300-acre estate.

The inn itself is the former corporate retreat of the Diamond Match company and provides an après-ski ambiance of rustic elegance and good evening meals. Skiers who want lunch can find food while on the trail into Lovell.

VAL HALLA COUNTRY CLUB AND
CROSS-COUNTRY SKI CENTER
Val Halla Road
Cumberland, Maine 04021
(207) 829-3700

Hours: 9 A.M. to 4 P.M.
Trail System: 25 kilometers (about 16 miles).
Trail Difficulty: Easiest, more difficult, most difficult.
Trail Grooming: Yes.
Rental Equipment: Yes.
Instruction: No.
Food Facilities: Snack bar and lounge at the Country Club; full
    restaurants within 15 miles.
Lodging: Hotels and motels within 10 miles.
How To Get There: Maine Turnpike to Exit 9; Route 1, Tuttle
Road, Middle Road, then Greely Road to Val Halla Road.

This touring center is a good example of the growing popularity
of country-club ski touring. An already established golf facility
turns nicely into a ski center with all the amenities and very
nice terrain for cross-country runs and tours. Val Halla is in the
Casco Bay region of the state, near both Portland and Freeport,
the now-famous home of L. L. Bean. The skiing itself is gentle
on the open flats, then rolling in the surrounding woods with
streams and ponds. In places the rolling terrain rolls into quite
a challenge for skiers of any level.

HARRIS FARM STAND SKI TOURING
Buzzel Road
Dayton, Maine 04005
(207) 499-2678

Hours: 8:30 A.M. to dusk.
Trail System: More than 30 kilometers (18 miles) of trails and
    open field skiing.
Trail Difficulty: Easiest, more difficult, most difficult.
Trail Grooming: Trails are groomed and trackset.

Rental Equipment: Yes.
Instruction: Yes.
Food Facilities: Snacks available in the warming shed.
Lodging: Inns in the region.
How to Get There: Take the Maine Turnpike to Kennebunk Exit, then follow Route 35 north. Turn right onto Gould Road, then right on Buzzell Road. Ski area will be on the right.

Harris Farm covers 500 acres of lovely rolling farmland and woods and offers a variety of open and sheltered skiing. Trails range from gentle beginner loops to steep rolling hills for advanced skiers. The forest is part of the American Tree Farm system and offers plenty of trail variety, from flatter wide trails to chutes and upland treks. Trails are nicely groomed throughout the winter. The area is near enough the tourist town of Kennebunkport to offer an excellent variety of lodging, dining, and shopping opportunities après-ski.

BEN-LOCH FARM SKI TOURING CENTER
RFD 1, North Road; Box 1020
Dixmont, Maine 04932
(207) 257-4768

Hours: 10 A.M. to dusk, seven days a week; night tours with headlamps.
Trail System: 38 kilometers (about 24 miles).
Trail Difficulty: Easiest, more difficult, most difficult.
Trail Grooming: Double trackset as needed; skating lanes.
Rental Equipment: 125 sets. Full retail shop.
Instruction: Individual and group; videotape sessions.
Food Facilities: Lunchroom at the center; group service by appointment; dinners.
Lodging: Bed-and-breakfast inns and motels within 10 miles.
How to Get There: Maine Turnpike to Exit 42 between Newport and Bangor, Maine; Route 143 east for 3½ miles to thé Ben-Loch sign; turn right.
The Ben-Loch Farm Ski Touring Center is a full-scale facility for serious workouts and every level of recreational touring. It offers

a well-maintained system of trail loops interlaced through the lovely Dixmont Hills country of east-central Maine. Beginners just getting their pins can stay for a while on the 10-acre field adjacent to the touring center. Here is where the instruction takes place. Then they can plunge into the 5-kilometer Penobscot Run, an intermediate trail that winds through deep woodlands and around a frozen pond. For the more adventurous, there is the St. John wilderness run or the Kennebec Loop. These are choppy twisters for the advanced skier.

Back at the center, there are a lunchroom, rental facilities, and a full retail shop that sells knickers, knee socks, hand-knit sweaters, and the like. Here, you can sign up for a night ski trip with headlamps and also pick up one of the best trail maps anywhere.

HOLLEY FARM RESORT
Holley Road
Farmington, Maine 04938
(207) 778-4869

Hours: December to April, 10:30 A.M. to 10:30 P.M. daily.
Trail System: 11 kilometers (about 6 miles); unlimited wilderness.
Trail Difficulty: Easiest, more difficult, most difficult.
Trail Grooming: Groomed and double trackset.
Rental Equipment: Yes.
Instruction: By appointment.
Food Facilities: Lunch and dinner at the farm.
Lodging: Several motels in the Farmington area. Trailside cabins.
How to Get There: Maine Turnpike to Exit 12, then Route 4 north to Farmington; pick up Holley Road for 1 mile to the center.

The field outside the Holley Farm center is a good warm-up for some good woods touring through the hardwood forest land of this region. It is a well-cared-for system that, although not large, offers good variety and some excellent training tracks. A

161

race program is being developed for the area, and all levels of recreational tourers will find comfortable ski surroundings here. The area also offers pool, sauna, restaurant, and lounge. New trailside cabins offer on-site housing.

TITCOMB MOUNTAIN SKI TOURING CENTER
Morrison Hill Road
Farmington, Maine 04938
(207) 778–9031

Hours: Tuesday through Friday, 1 to 4 P.M.; Saturday and Sunday, 9 A.M. to 4 P.M.
Trail System: 25 kilometers (about 15 miles); unlimited wilderness.

162

Trail Difficulty: Easiest, more difficult, most difficult.
Trail Grooming: Yes.
Rental Equipment: Nearby in Farmington.
Instruction: Yes.
Food Facilities: Lunch available at the lodge; several restaurants nearby.
Lodging: Several inns and motels in the area.
How to Get There: Maine Turnpike to the Auburn, Maine, exit; Route 4 north to Farmington.

In the foothills of the Longfellow Mountains in west-central Maine, the Titcomb trails—mostly beginner and intermediate—roll over gentle hills and through meadows and fir forest. The trail system accesses an additional 15 miles of trails in the woods, one of them leading to a downtown restaurant in this pretty college-campus town. Through the Farmington Ski Club, Titcomb offers citizen racing, ski jumping, and Telemark practice on the nearby Alpine area. The large lodge has a lunch counter, rest rooms, and changing and waxing rooms. Lessons are given each afternoon, by appointment.

TROLL VALLEY CROSS-COUNTRY CENTER
Red Schoolhouse Road
Farmington, Maine 04938
(207) 778-3656

Hours: 9 A.M. to dusk.
Trail System: 25 kilometers (about 16 miles).
Trail Difficulty: Easiest, more difficult, most difficult.
Trail Grooming: All trails groomed and trackset.
Rental Equipment: Yes.
Instruction: Yes.
Food Facilities: Lunch counter and dining room.
Lodging: Inns in the area.
How to Get There: Get off Route 95 at Auburn, and follow Route 4 to Farmington. Between Wilton and Farmington Centers, Red Schoolhouse Roads runs off Route 4 to the left.

Established in 1985 as a cross-country and fitness center, Troll Valley is in the snowbelt of Western Maine, keeping it operating on an average of 105 days per winter. The trail network is laid out over about 300 acres of what was once rolling farmland. Replacing the old farmhouse is a modern lodge with food and equipment service, replete with a crackling fire. The trails vary from open-field skiing to beaver bogs and cedar swamps. The rolling hillsides offer some very challenging up- and downhill treks, and all trails are wide enough (12 to 20 feet) for a track along the sides with skating in the middle of the trail.

Off-trail skiing is nearly limitless at this area, and the adventurous skier finds himself in the foothills of the Longfellow Mountains with spectacular views of these hills and the flatlands of the Sandy River Plantation.

CRAB APPLE INN
The Forks, Maine 04985
(207) 663-2218

Hours: No set hours.
Trail System: About 95 kilometers (about 55 miles); access to unlimited wilderness.
Trail Difficulty: Easiest, more difficult, most difficult.
Trail Grooming: None, except by snowmobiles that use the area.
Rental Equipment: None.
Instruction: No.
Food Facilities: Breakfast and dinner by reservation at the inn; lunch snacks at the nearby general store.
Lodging: Seven rooms at the inn; housekeeping cottage.
How to Get There: Maine Turnpike to Exit 36; Route 201 for 62 miles to The Forks.

Overlooking a dramatic sweep of the Kennebec River, Crab Apple Inn offers seven rooms as well as a guest house with housekeeping privileges. This is North Country skiing in the true sense of that term, as the old logging roads here criss-cross infinitely, it seems, through deep wilderness forest, along the

river valley, and up over mountain ridges along the trail along
which Benedict Arnold marched his troops to Quebec. That
wonderful city, incidentally, is just 140 miles from the inn.
   Everyone at some point should have the experience of skiing into Moxie Falls—the highest waterfall in New England—or
explore The Forks itself, a point of land at the confluence of the
Dead and Kennebec rivers. Available from the inn are guided
backcountry tours where trekkers cannot help but run across
signs of snowshoe hare, deer, and moose. This is not for experts
only, by the way, as the riverside trails along the Kennebec are
gentle and groomed out by snowmobiles. This is true New England wilderness skiing several light years from civilization. In
summer, it is a marvelous white-water rafting center.

CHESUNCOOK LAKE HOUSE
Chesuncook Village
Route 76, Box 655
Greenville, Maine 04441
(207) 695-2821 (Folsom's Flying Service)

Hours: By arrangement.
Trail System: Infinite.
Trail Difficulty: Easiest, more difficult, most difficult.
Trail Grooming: No.
Rental Equipment: No
Instruction: For tour groups only.
Food Facilities: Dinner only.
Lodging: Housekeeping cabins are available and well equipped;
   bring sleeping bags and food.
How to Get There: No auto access; visitors must ski, sled, or
   fly in; make contact through Folsom's Flying Service.

Chesuncook is another of the prime wilderness ski-guide outfitters that can put together an outback trek for all tastes and
abilities of skiing. The Chesuncook Lake House Lodge and
Cabins is a well-established fishing complex in the remote uplands of central Maine. In winter, Chesuncook offers the serious skier an opportunity to enjoy the solitude and seclusion of

165

the northern Maine experience. This is a remote, primitive area for advanced skiers or for those folks flexible enough to approach such an experience with respect, understanding, and foresight. Skiers who do are rewarded with the truly amazing experiences of this country, from the "quiet beauty of the sun igniting the ice crystals on Baxter Peak in the early morn, to the pristine solitude of a snow-covered landscape with the vast open spaces of the frozen lakes . . ."—lines penned by a frequent skier at Chesuncook. It may not be easy to reach, but that is part of the charm. For real wilderness skiing, it's worth the hassle of getting here.

MOUNTAIN VIEW FARM CROSS-COUNTRY SKI CENTER
Big Squaw Mountain
Greenville, Maine 04441
(207) 695–2272 or 1–800–MSHD

Hours: 9 A.M. to 4 P.M. daily.
Trail System: 45 kilometers (about 28 miles).
Trail Difficulty: Easiest, more difficult, most difficult.
Trail Grooming: 15 kilometers groomed and trackset; unlimited wilderness skiing.
Rental Equipment: Yes.
Instruction: Yes.
Food Facilities: Lunches in the cafeteria, with lunches and dinners in main lodge.
Lodging: Fifty-five separate units in the main lodge; the bunkroom sleeps forty dormitory-style.
How to Get There: I–95 to Newport, Maine; Route 7 north to Dexter; Route 23 north to Guilford; Routes 6 and 15 north to Greenville, signs to Squaw Mountain.

Though remote, the Squaw Mountain Touring Center shares the complete facilities of the Alpine area, so skiers here can enjoy après-ski hours in relative luxury. The interlacing trail loops over 45 kilometers, with nearly limitless possibilities encompassed in the trails and logging roads that maze throughout the Moosehead Lake Region. One loop goes across and around the frozen water; another leads skiers up to a wonderful panoramic overlook of this huge lake. Then a call to Dick Folsom at Folsom's Flying Service in Greenville will get you a fly-in ski trek to the Allagash or Baxter areas for some remote wilderness skiing. At Squaw itself, Telemarking and Alpine are also available, as are all the amenities of rental, retail, food, and lounging facilities.

SPRUCE MOUNTAIN CROSS-COUNTRY CENTER
RFD 2, Box 8425
Jay, Maine 04239
(207) 897–0490

Hours: Dawn to dusk, December to April.
Trail System: 15 kilometers (about 9 miles).
Trail Difficulty: Easiest, more difficult, most difficult.
Trail Grooming: Groomed and trackset; skating lanes.
Rental Equipment: No.
Instruction: No.
Food Facilities: At the Alpine hill.
Lodging: In the Farmington area or Lewiston area, within 10 to 18 miles.
How to Get There: Maine Turnpike to Exit 12; Route 4 north, turn right before the bridge into Livermore Falls. The center is ½ mile down the river.

Spruce Mountain is a small area run in conjunction with the Spruce Mountain Alpine area on the west bank of the Androscoggin River. When the Alpine slopes are in operation, a snack bar is available. The trails vary in length and difficulty, from rolling riverside roadways to some challenging up-and-down loops that provide Alpine trails for Telemarking.

WINTER'S INN SKI TOURING CENTER
Box 44
Kingfield, Maine 04947
(207) 265–5421

Hours: 9 A.M. to dusk.
Trail System: 30 kilometers (about 19 miles).
Trail Difficulty: Easiest, more difficult.
Trail Grooming: No.
Rental Equipment: Yes.
Instruction: No.
Food Facilities: Breakfast and dinner at the inn; lunches within skiing distance of the center.
Lodging: Winter's Inn has twelve rooms; several motels and inns in the area.
How to Get There: Maine Turnpike to the second Augusta exit; Route 27 north to Kingfield.

Here, in one of the most dramatic mountain areas in the Northeast—the Bigelow Range overlooking the Carrabassett Valley—Winter's Inn sits on a small hilltop overlooking the village of Kingfield. This restored Victorian country mansion was originally designed by the Stanley Brothers who invented the Stanley Steamer. It has five working fireplaces, a genial atmosphere, and plenty of art objects and antiques to look at. The inn overlooks Bigelow, Mt. Abrams, and Mt. Blue, as well as one of New England's true classic Alpine areas, Sugarloaf/USA.

Skiers have nearly limitless terrain at their disposal on wilderness trails carved from old logging roads, down through pine glades to the West Branch of the Carrabassett River. Here the wildlife is abundant, the skiing varied and vigorous. There is also open-field skiing through gently rolling uplands. For Telemark aficionados, Sugarloaf has plenty of terrain both gentle and steep. This big-country region can be skied season after season without giving up all her secrets and surprises to skiers.

MOUNT ABRAM SKI TOURING
Box 193
Locke Mills, Maine 04255
(207) 875-2601

Hours: 9 A.M. to 4 P.M.
Trail System: 14 kilometers (about 9 miles).
Trail Difficulty: Easiest, more difficult, most difficult.
Trail Grooming: Groomed and trackset; no skating.
Rental Equipment: Yes.
Instruction: By appointment.
Food Facilities: Cafeteria for lunches in the lodge.
Lodging: In Bethel or West Paris, about 10 miles away.
How to Get There: Maine Turnpike to Exit 11, then Route 26
   to Locke Mills.

Mt. Abram Ski Touring center is nestled beside Alpine slopes, allowing skiers to make use of Telemark terrain, as well as the skier facilities already there. After skiing along the base of the downhill slopes, tourers plunge into the snow-laden hardwood and pine trails, following old logging roads, stream beds, and small bridges crisscrossing Putt Brook. This is picturesque terrain, easy to negotiate, though there are some challenging climbs, twists, turns, and descents on some of the trails. Moonlight tours are available along a wide trail, and citizen races are encouraged here, including the annual Bob Cole Cup Race.

BAXTER STATE PARK
64 Balsam Drive
Millinocket, Maine 04462
(207) 723-5140

Hours: Daylight, December through March.
Trail System: Wilderness trails in a 100-square-mile tract.
Trail Difficulty: Easiest, more difficult, most difficult.
Trail Grooming: None.
Rental Equipment: No.
Instruction: No.

Food Facilities: In Millinocket, about 25 miles away.
Lodging: In Millinocket.
How to Get There: I-95 to Millinocket, then Greenville Road
to the Baxter State Park entrance 18 miles past town.

Though Baxter State Park is on a well-worn path of Maine's
summertime delights, in winter, it is a remote wild land of
fierce weather and tough outdoor challenges. Thus, touring
here should be considered only by the most experienced woods-
man-skier who has a working knowledge of what winter means
in this deep northern country (though the skiing itself need not
be the hairest, especially with the miles of flattish logging
roads between Millinocket and Greenville). Winter camping is
available in a limited number of bunkhouses, lean-tos, tents,
and igloos. Skiers must either bushwhack in to the Park Headquarters, or take the Golden Road, sharing it with lumber carri-
ers bringing pulp wood to the mill.

All the caveats aside, however, this is wonderful back-
woods country along one of the most spectacular watercourses
in the Northeast—the West Branch of the Penobscot River. The
snow-covered bulk of Mt. Katahdin looms over the land (it may
not be climbed in winter, incidentally). For skiers who truly
want to break away from the crowds, and who are confident of
their outdoor skills, Baxter State Park is among the finest
wilderness ski expeditions to be found anywhere.

KATAHDIN LAKE WILDERNESS CAMPS
Box 389
Millinocket, Maine 04462

Hours: Daily, dawn to dusk.
Trail System: 48 kilometers (30 miles).
Trail Difficulty: More difficult, most difficult wilderness trails.
Trail Grooming: No.
Rental Equipment: No.
Instruction: No.
Food Facilities: Yes.
Lodging: At the camp center and camps.

171

How to Get There: I–95 to Route 157 to Millinocket Lake. Here, either fly-in or ski-in access; there is no auto road.

On the remote shores of Katahdin Lake, these wilderness camps are the gateway to real outback trekking experience. Like many such guided tours, skiing skill and experience are not the critical factors. Rather, Katahdin's tours are for adventurous folks in fairly good physical shape who are flexible enough to trade amenities for stunning wilderness adventure. Being in decent shape, though, is a starter.

The tour begins with a fly-in (or ski-in) to the camps along the frozen shore of the beautiful Katahdin Lake, about 30 miles north of Millinocket. If you ski from the lake, where you'll leave your car, to the camps, it is a full-day, 20-mile trek. However, Scotty's Flying Service at Shin Pond will be happy to take you in. It takes about twelve minutes by plane.

At the camp center there are American Plan accommodations with family-style meals. Aside from this there are no rental or retail goods available, so skiers must bring what is necessary for a few days of trekking—from clothes and equipment to waxes. One tip: Bring a camera. You'll be touring in some of the most astounding backcountry anywhere, a place where "the only nightlife you will hear will be a distant owl or coyote in the hills," in the words of director Al Cooper. In the morning the tracks of a grouse, moose, or pine marten crossing your trail may tell you are not completely alone in this beautiful winter world.

CARTER'S FARM MARKET SKI TOURING CENTER
Route 26
Oxford, Maine 04270
(207) 539–4848

Hours: 9 A.M. to 6 P.M. Night skiing on weekends.
Trail System: 20 kilometers (about 12 miles).
Trail Difficulty: Easiest, more difficult.
Trail Grooming: Groomed and trackset; skating lanes.
Rental Equipment: Yes; retail shop.

Instruction: Yes.
Food Facilities: Trail snacks at center; restaurants within a few
  miles.
Lodging: Motels in South Paris and Otisfield, about 7 miles
  away. Bed-and-breakfast available at center.
How to Get There: Maine Turnpike through Portland, Maine,
  to Exit 11 at Gray. Route 100 to Route 26 north. The farm
  is about 12 miles from Gray.

So many of the most pleasant New England touring centers
have been established on working farms, and this one is in that
tradition. Carter's Farm Market is a summer produce operation
which, once the snow flies, turns its gently rolling pastureland
and woods into a full-scale touring center. The retail/rental facility is well stocked with skis, clothing, and equipment, and
the lodge is a friendly place to relax and talk about what wax
you should have used.

   The trails at Carter Farm are varied, from open-field cruis-
ers and racing courses, to one lovely solitary tour along the Androscoggin River. Hogan's Pond is another pretty destination
for a daily tour. At the Carters', citizen races are run throughout the season, along with junior programs and a Winter Carnival. Night skiing is also a fun feature of the area. David Carter,
director of the area, is a cross-country skier with twenty-five
years' experience who set up the Jackson Touring Center for
Eastern Mountain Sports. When it comes to running a touring
center, Carter knows what he is about.

SADDLEBACK
Box 490
Rangeley, Maine 04970
(207) 864–5671

Hours: 9 A.M. to 4 P.M.
Trail System: 40 kilometers (25 miles).
Trail Difficulty: Easiest, more difficult, most difficult.
Trail Grooming: As needed; 35 kilometers groomed; skating
  lanes.

Rental Equipment: Yes.
Instruction: PSIA-certified instructors; Telemark.
Food Facilities: Available at the Saddleback Mountain base lodge.
Lodging: Condominiums available at the mountain; inns and motels in the town nearby.
How to Get There: Maine Turnpike to Exit 12 in Auburn, Maine; Route 4 north to Rangeley; follow signs to Saddleback and the touring facility.

As an Alpine area, Saddleback is rightfully dubbed New England's best-kept secret. The same can be said for the Nordic touring center and the region generally. It is a land of broad lakes—Rangeley, Saddleback, and Mooselookmeguntik—and trout streams that course out of the Bigelow Mountains, whose peaks command views of the entire region. Despite the beauty of the area and a base elevation (2,500 feet) that ensures a much longer-than-average ski season, the Rangeley region is uncrowded and unhurried. This is a perfect area to combine a Nordic-Alpine ski vacation, or to make use of Saddleback Mountain's easier Alpine trails for your Telemark work. The 40 kilometers of carefully groomed and trackset trails combine all the terrain, from gentle rolling tours along the lake shore, and across the lake expanse, to stiff climbs up the flank of Saddleback Mountain itself. One reward for this climb is a truly stunning view of Saddleback Lake followed by a gentle meandering descent down the Lazy River trail. Then follow this with an après-ski hour in the Painted Pony, Saddleback's rollicking lounge upstairs at the base lodge. A full cafeteria operates daily here and serves a homemade chili that must, hands down, take top chili honors in all of ski land.

THE BIRCHES SKI TOURING CENTER
Rockwood, Maine 04478
(207) 534–7305

Hours: Dawn to dusk.
Trail System: 40 kilometers (25 miles); unlimited wilderness.
Trail Difficulty: Easiest, more difficult, most difficult.

Trail Grooming: Groomed and trackset as needed.
Rental Equipment: Yes.
Instruction: PSIA-certified.
Food Facilities: Restaurant in Rockwood Center, 2 miles from the center.
Lodging: Several cabins and lodges in the area.
How to Get There: I-95 to Newport, Maine, then Route 7 north to Dexter; Route 23 north to Guilford; pick up Routes 6 and 15 through the town of Greenville around the lake to Rockwood; cross the Moose River and follow a logging road to center.

Looking for wilderness ski trips? Overnights? Fly-ins to the wild backcountry of the Northeast? Here it is. Maine's big North Woods is the closest thing in New England to rival Michigan's Upper Peninsula. This is not intended to scare off less-experienced skiers but simply to remind potential visitors that outback trekking in this countryside requires forethought, planning, and investigation. That said, the rewards of skiing The Birches are immense, and the sport enters an entirely new dimension.

The center itself overlooks Mt. Kineo, and skiers can be content to stay on the 40 kilometers of groomed, trackset trails along the picturesque western shore of the lake. There is a rental and retail shop, and hot drinks and sandwiches are available. For the adventurous, The Birches operates in conjunction with North Country Outfitters and can plan a multiday trek for skiers; the only requirements are good health and a willing heart. No experience is necessary, in other words. You will be in the hands of professional guides and instructors who will lead the tour through these stupendous backlands, leaving 2,000-foot towers like Elephant and Indian mountains at your back. During the day, you'll ski from inn to inn along old logging roads and woodland trails; late in the afternoon you'll be ready to relax around a warm store before the big home-cooked dinner at the inn.

For the ultimate New England trek, The Birches offers a backpacking tour to Chimney Pond at the base of mile-high Mt. Katahdin. By day you'll be working over Alpine terrain— rock faces, ice falls, and snow fields. You'll learn the basics of

winter mountaineering and ski the lower snow bowls of the
majestic Katahdin. This trip requires both physical and mental
stamina, though not great skiing experience. The adventure is
well worth the effort.

BLACK MOUNTAIN OF MAINE
50 Congress Street
Rumford, Maine 04276
(207) 364–8977

Hours: Dawn to dusk, December through March.
Trail System: 15 kilometers (about 9 miles).
Trail Difficulty: Easiest, more difficult, most difficult.
Trail Grooming: Groomed and trackset.
Rental Equipment: Nearby in Rumford.
Instruction: Yes.
Food Facilities: A lunch counter at the center.
Lodging: In Rumford.
How to Get There: Maine Turnpike north to Auburn; Route 4
    to Livermore; Route 108 to Rumford.

Black Mountain of Maine is a medium-sized area in the central
range of the state, near an Alpine ski area and ski-jumping complex. The trail system was intelligently designed by Chammy
Broomhall, designer of the Olympic trail system at Lake Placid
and Squaw Valley, and still a vital part of the competitive
Nordic scene. Black Mountain reflects this dedication to high-
quality cross-country skiing on every level, from first-time-out
novices to racers training for a Ski Chase marathon.

Index to Skiing Sites

A

Acadia National Park (Bar Harbor, Maine), 151
Alpine Haven (Montgomery Center, Vermont), 89
AMC Pinkham Notch Camp (Gorham, New Hampshire), 130
Ascutney Mountain Resort Touring Center (Brownsville, Vermont), 68

B

Balsams Wilderness, The (Dixville Notch, New Hampshire), 123
Baxter State Park (Millinocket, Maine), 169
Ben-Loch Farm Ski Touring Center (Dixmont, Maine), 160
Bethel Inn Ski Touring Center (Bethel, Maine), 152
Birches Ski Touring Center, The (Rockwood, Maine), 174
Birch Hill Inn (Manchester, Vermont), 87
Black Mountain of Maine (Rumford, Maine), 176
Blueberry Hill (Goshen, Vermont), 75
Bolton Valley Cross Country Center (Bolton, Vermont), 65
Brattleboro Outing Club Ski Hut (Brattleboro, Vermont), 67
Bretton Woods Ski Touring Center (Bretton Woods, New Hampshire), 120
Brodie Mountain Ski Resort (New Ashford, Massachusetts), 51
Bucksteep Manor Cross-Country Ski Center (Washington, Massachusetts), 55
Burke Mountain Ski Touring Center (East Burke, Vermont), 74
Butternut Ski Touring (Great Barrington, Massachusetts), 48

C

Camel's Hump Nordic Ski Center (Huntington, Vermont), 78
Cannon Mountain (Franconia, New Hampshire), 128
Canoe Meadows Wildlife Sanctuary (Pittsfield, Massachusetts), 53
Carrabassett Valley Recreation Center (Carrabassett Valley, Maine), 157
Carrol and Jane Rikert Ski Touring Center (Middlebury, Vermont), 89
Carter's Cross-Country Ski Area (Bethel, Maine), 153
Carter's Farm Market Ski Touring Center (Oxford, Maine), 172
Catamount Family Center (Williston, Vermont), 108
Catamount Trail Association, The (Burlington, Vermont), 69

Cedar Brook Farms Cross-Country Ski Center (West Suffield, Connecticut), 39
Chesuncook Lake House (Greenville, Maine), 165
Churchill House Inn and Ski Touring Center (Brandon, Vermont), 66
Crab Apple Inn (The Forks, Maine), 164
Craftsbury Nordic Ski Center (Craftsbury Common, Vermont), 73
Cross-Country Skiing and Snowshoeing in Wayland (Wayland, Massachusetts), 56

D
Darby Field Inn, The (Conway, New Hampshire), 122
Deer Cap Ski Touring Center (Ossipee, New Hampshire), 139

E
Eastman Ski Touring Center (Grantham, New Hampshire), 131
East Mountain Ski Touring Center (Westfield, Massachusetts), 56
Edson Hill Manor (Stowe, Vermont), 98

F
Fox Run Resort (Ludlow, Vermont), 86
Franconia Inn Cross-Country Ski Center (Franconia, New Hampshire), 129

G
Grafton Ponds Cross-Country Ski Center (Grafton, Vermont), 76
Great Brook Farm Ski Touring Center (Carlisle, Massachusetts), 44
Green Mountain Touring Center (Randolph, Vermont), 95
Green Trails Inn & Ski Touring Center (Brookfield, Vermont), 67
Gunstock Cross-Country Center (Laconia, New Hampshire), 135

H
Harris Farm Stand Ski Touring (Dayton, Maine), 159
Hazen's Notch Ski Touring Center (Montgomery Center, Vermont), 91
Heermansmith Farm (Irasburg [Coventry Village], Vermont), 79
Hermitage Cross-Country Touring Center (Wilmington, Vermont), 109
Hickory Hill Touring Center (Worthington, Massachusetts), 60
Highland Lodge (Greensboro, Vermont), 77

Hildene Ski Touring Center (Manchester, Vermont), 88
Hilltop Cross-Country Center (Wolcott, Vermont), 113
Holley Farm Resort (Farmington, Maine), 161

I

Inn at East Hill Farm, The (Troy, New Hampshire), 144
Inn at Quail Run (Wilmington, Vermont), 110
Intervale Nordic Ski Touring Center (Intervale, New Hampshire), 132

J

Jackson Ski Touring Foundation (Jackson, New Hampshire), 132
Jay Peak Ski Area (Jay, Vermont), 80

K

Katahdin Lake Wilderness Camps (Millinocket, Maine), 171
Kennedy Park (Lenox, Massachusetts), 49

L

Lincoln Guide Service (Lincoln, Massachusetts), 50
Little Lyford Pond Lodge (Brownville, Maine), 155
Loon Mountain Cross-Country Center (Lincoln, New Hampshire), 136

M

Maple Corner Farm Cross-Country Ski Area (Granville,
    Massachusetts), 47
Montpelier Elks Ski Touring Center, The (Montpelier, Vermont), 92
Moose Mountain Lodge (Etna, New Hampshire), 126
Mount Abram Ski Touring (Locke Mills, Maine), 169
Mt. Mansfield Touring Center (Stowe, Vermont), 99
Mountain Meadows Ski Touring Center (Killington, Vermont), 83
Mountain Top Ski Touring Center (Chittenden, Vermont), 72
Mountain View Farm Cross-Country Ski Center (Greenville, Maine), 166

N

Natanis Cross-Country Ski Trails (Augusta, Maine), 150
Nordic Adventures (Rochester, Vermont), 96
Nordic Inn Ski Touring Center (Landgrove, Vermont), 84
Nordic Skier, The (Wolfeboro, New Hampshire), 146
Norsk Cross-Country Ski Center (New London, New Hampshire), 138
North Country Ski Touring Center (Carlisle, Massachusetts), 45
Northfield Mountain Ski Touring Center (Northfield, Massachusetts), 52
Notchview Reservation (Windsor, Massachusetts), 59

O

Oak n' Spruce Resort (South Lee, Massachusetts), 54
Ole's Cross Country (Warren, Vermont), 105

P

Perry Hollow Cross-Country Center (New Durham,
     New Hampshire), 137
Pine Mountain Ski Touring Center (East Hartland, Connecticut), 36
Prospect Mountain Ski Touring Center (Old Bennington, Vermont), 93

Q

Quinebaug Valley Ski Touring Center (Norwich, Connecticut), 38

R

Rabbit Hill Inn (Lower Waterford, Vermont), 85
Red Fox Ski Touring Center (Jeffersonville, Vermont), 81
Road's End Farm (Chesterfield, New Hampshire), 121
Rolling Green Ski Touring Center (Andover, Massachusetts), 44

S

Saddleback (Rangeley, Maine), 173
Shattuck Inn Nordic Ski Center (Jackson, New Hampshire), 134
Sitzmark Lodge (Wilmington, Vermont), 111
Ski Tours of Vermont (Chester, Vermont), 70
Snorada Recreation Center (Auburn, Maine), 156
Snowvillage Inn (Snowville, New Hampshire), 141

Spruce Mountain Cross-Country Center (Jay, Maine), 167
Sterling Ridge Inn (Jeffersonville, Vermont), 82
Stratton Mountain Cross-Country Center (Stratton Mountain,
    Vermont), 103
Sugarbush Inn/Rossignol Ski Touring Center (Warren, Vermont), 106
Sunday River Cross-Country Ski Center (Bethel, Maine), 154
Sunset Hill Touring Center (Sugar Hill, New Hampshire), 142
Swift River Inn (Cummington, Massachusetts), 46

T
Tater Hill Cross-Country Ski Center (Chester, Vermont), 71
Temple Mountain Ski Touring (Peterborough, New Hampshire), 140
Timber Creek Ski Touring Center (West Dover, Vermont), 107
Titcomb Mountain Ski Touring Center (Farmington, Maine), 162
Topnotch Touring Center (Stowe, Vermont), 100
Tory Pines (Francestown, New Hampshire), 127
Trail Head Ski Touring (Stockbridge, Vermont), 97
Trapp Family Lodge (Stowe, Vermont), 102
Troll Valley Lodge Ski Touring Center (Farmington, Maine), 163
Tucker Hill Ski Touring Center (Waitsfield, Vermont), 104

V
Val Halla Country Club and Cross-Country Ski Center (Cumberland,
    Maine), 159
Valley View Country Club (Dunbarton, New Hampshire), 125
Vermont Voyager Expeditions (Montgomery Center, Vermont), 92
Viking Ski Touring Centre (Londonderry, Vermont), 85

W
Wachusett Mountain Ski Area (Princeton, Massachusetts), 53
Waterville Valley Cross-Country Ski Area (Waterville Valley,
    New Hampshire), 145
West Mountain Inn, The (Arlington, Vermont), 64
Weston Ski Track (Weston, Massachusetts), 58
Westways on Kezar Lake (Center Lovell, Maine), 158
White House Touring Center, The (Wilmington, Vermont), 112
White Memorial Foundation (Litchfield, Connecticut), 37
Wilderness Trails and Nordic Ski School (Quechee, Vermont), 94

Wild Wings Ski Touring Center (Peru, Vermont), 94
Windblown Ski Touring (New Ipswich, New Hampshire), 138
Windham Hill Inn & Touring Center (West Townshend, Vermont), 107
Winding Trails Ski Touring Center (Farmington, Connecticut), 36
Winter's Inn Ski Touring Center (Kingfield, Maine), 168
Woodbound Inn (Jaffrey, New Hampshire), 135
Woodstock Ski Touring Center (Woodstock, Vermont), 114